A MILLION TINY STEPS

From Refugee to Physician in South Sudan

HELLEN ONYANGO
WITH LORI WINDSOR MOHR

Published October 2020

Printed in the United States of America

Print ISBN: 978-0-578-75133-7

Library of Congress Control Number:

Santa Barbara Literary Press

ALSO BY LORI WINDSOR MOHR

Novels

THE ROAD AT MY DOOR

THE WORLD ON A STRING

Memoirs

NO ORDINARY LIFE

CHILD SOLDIER

Short Stories

THE LUCY CHRONICLES

THE SEARCH FOR LIFE, 9/11

A MILLION TINY STEPS

From Refugee to Physician

BY HELLEN ONYANGO
WITH LORI WINDSOR MOHR

For Likali

"Everything can be taken from a man but one thing: the last of human freedoms—to choose one's attitude in any given set of circumstances, to choose one's own way."

Viktor Frankl, *Man's Search for Meaning*

CONTENTS

South Sudan, Africa

North and South Sudan

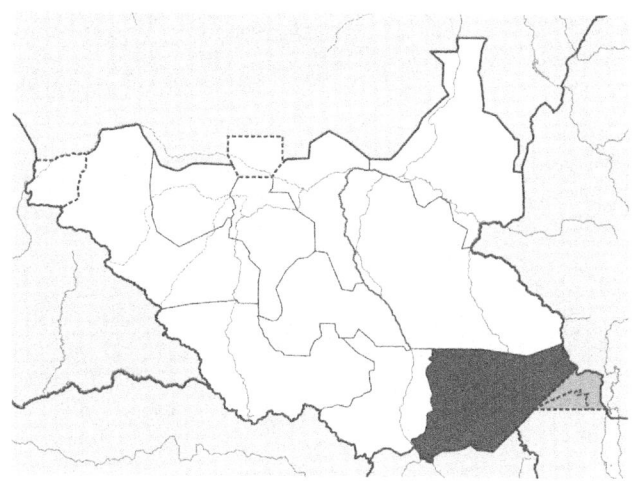

Eastern Equitoria State

Hellen's birthplace, Lafon, Eastern Equitoria State

FOREWORD
Kenneth Waxman, M.D.

Dr. Waxman, Gogrial, South Sudan, 2010

I was overjoyed to see that Hellen has now told her story. It is a story that is at once tragic, awe-inspiring, and heroic. When you read Hellen's story, you will see.

I first travelled to South Sudan in 2010, just before it became our world's newest nation. I had the opportunity to work there as a surgeon with *Doctors without Borders*. I expected to have the usual experience of a western doctor working in underdeveloped nations—seeing patients with lots of interesting diseases and feeling good about helping. But living in South Sudan affected me much more profoundly than I ever imagined. I had entered what is probably the most under-served medical country in the world. The needs were overwhelming, and the access to modern care was most often non-existing. South Sudan has suffered countless decades of oppression and war; it has experienced few of the benefits of modern medical care. Countless South Sudanese suffer and die of preventable and treatable infections, countless mothers and babies die during childbirth, countless children die of common diseases such as diarrhea, countless citizens do not receive treatment after injuries, and develop terrible and unnecessary consequences such as infections and amputations. I was devastated to witness indescribable suffering and death.

But there was hope! In 2011 South Sudan became an independent nation. Its people and the world were jubilant with optimism that progress would finally begin. But tragically, this has not occurred. After a decade of independence, South Sudan remains embroiled in political turmoil, unending violence, and economic disaster. Medical care has not improved. The ravages of poverty, malnutrition, disease, suffering and death in South Sudan are worse than ever.

One would expect that the people in this type of hostile environment would be downtrodden and dejected....even more so, because the people of South Sudan have been hunted and oppressed for hundreds of years. But this is not the case. I have been amazed and inspired to witness the unwavering resilience of the South Sudanese people. With deep faith and spirituality, the South Sudanese meet their challenges face on, with resolve and optimism. The cultures of tribal South Sudan are ancient; they are closely tied to reliance upon their land and the natural environment. And as children of these cultures, South Sudanese have learned self-reliance and self-preservation. They are strong, they are stoic, and they have inspiring depth of character. When you read Hellen's story, you will see.

A major obstacle to medical progress in South Sudan is that there are very few South Sudanese health care providers. Medical education has not been functional for decades. Most trained South Sudanese doctors have left the country. To try to do something to help, I began a small non-profit organization—*Future Doctors for South Sudan*—in 2011 to help a few South Sudanese students attend medical school in Kenya and Uganda. Hellen was one of our applicants. With the help of friends and family, we have now helped fifteen South Sudanese students receive medical education. It is a tiny number. But our hope is that when our students return to their country to provide modern healthcare, they will not only help countless patients, but also serve as examples that others will follow. The individuals we have chosen to support are all amazing. They have all overcome unthinkable obstacles to not only receive education, but to excel. They have all endured great hardships and have sacrificed greatly in Herculean quests to become doctors.

Hellen is one of our students. She overcame unthinkable obstacles to complete her medical education and has now returned to South Sudan to help her people. As a woman in a country with an astounding rate of illiteracy for women, Hellen's challenges were even more daunting. But Hellen has the strength of a heroine, the courage of a lioness, and the heart of a physician. When you read her story, you will see.

Dr. Kenneth Waxman is a physician board certified in surgery and surgical critical care.

Dr. Waxman with a medical student in Gogrial, 2010

Me kneading sorghum as a girl.

Me (right) with my father and siblings.

1

CROSSING THE THRESHOLD

Nyal, South Sudan

The door falls shut behind me, aluminum making a soft clang as it settles into the frame. Slipping off my sandals, I drop on the bed. Just fifteen minutes, that's all I need to decompress. In California it's the middle of the night. The time difference with South Sudan gives me a chance to think before I respond to Lori's email. She wants to write a book about me, about my life growing up during the war— the Second Sudanese Civil War—as one of those who survived and went on to live some semblance of the life we might have dreamed of as children.

How can I explain such a story to a sixty-something white woman in southern California? What common language can we find to bridge the enormous gulf between our worlds? All she knows about me is what she has read in my bio on the *Future Doctors for South Sudan* website, which isn't much. I am grateful to Dr. Ken for all he has done for me and the other students. Without his nonprofit I would not be here, resting on my bed in Nyal in charge of this rural clinic, my first paying job as a doctor since finishing medical school in Nairobi at Mount Kenya University.

How I connected with Dr. Ken is a tale of good luck. The global nonprofit, *Doctors without Borders*, had sent a team of physicians to Gogrial in South Sudan in the fall of 2010. Dr. Ken, a surgeon from California, was among them. The civil war had officially ended between government forces in northern Sudan and the Sudanese People's Liberation Army in the south in 2005, but the peace agreement failed. The fighting continued. Gogrial was not the safest of places when Dr. Ken arrived with the *Doctors without Borders* team. It would be another year before southern Sudan gained independence from the north to become the world's newest nation, The Republic of South Sudan.

Dr. Ken's time in Gogrial had a profound impact on him, one that would eventually result in a lifeline for me. When he returned to the United States, Dr. Ken decided that he wanted to help my country. The patients he had treated in the rural clinic, the distances from which they traveled to get there, mostly on foot, made it clear that access to healthcare was a major issue undermining our health. People in rural villages simply have no clinic services—that is, without walking long distances, sometimes days, carrying their loved one or neighbor who needs medical help. Access to care is the major reason our mortality rate is so high.

In South Sudan with our government in tatters after twenty-two years of civil war, we have been relying on non-governmental organizations—NGOs, like *Doctors without Borders*—to provide healthcare. But nonprofits come and go. Most trained physicians leave South Sudan after medical school for opportunities elsewhere. Dr. Ken's nonprofit aimed at supporting the healthcare system from the ground up with doctors who would remain in the country after completing their educations.

That has been another hurdle for med students. The educational system in South Sudan is almost as dismal as the healthcare, in complete disarray after two decades of war. Widespread poverty also meant that students already in the medical school pipeline often stalled before graduating when the funding dried up. That was me. How I got to medical school in the first place is another story, the one Dr. Ken's friend, Lori, wants me to tell. When I think what a long hard road it would have been in normal times, it is nothing short of astounding that I got through medical school at all. War has been a constant in my life, along with the hardships brought by poverty and a government struggling to get on its feet. In our vast country most roads are not paved. During the rainy season, I have driven countless muddy ones getting from Point A to Point B. My journey to medical school was like walking those roads in boots of lead, every step a phenomenal effort driven by fierce determination.

Mine is a story of success in a country where lack of a functioning system of higher education puts success out of reach for most of those lucky enough to make it that far. So I understand Lori's wanting me to write about it. Where would I even begin? My life has been defined by two opposing forces—relentless war, and the pursuit of education. School has been the saving grace of my existence, war the obstacle to achieving it. When I was born, the illiteracy rate in southern Sudan for girls was 88%. In the 1990s and early 2000s, getting an education of any kind was still intensely difficult. In the twenty first century it is slightly easier, but even today less than one percent of girls completes her primary education.

My success has been even more unlikely as a member of the Pari tribe located at the foot of the Lafon hills of Eastern Equitoria State where our ancestors have lived for generations. Formal education was never part of our tradition. A pastoral people with deep ties to the land, elders handed their knowledge down to their children, who then passed it on to their children, one generation to the next learning what they needed, which was not in any book. Life might have continued like that had South Sudan not been involved in two civil wars. The second one is the backdrop to my story.

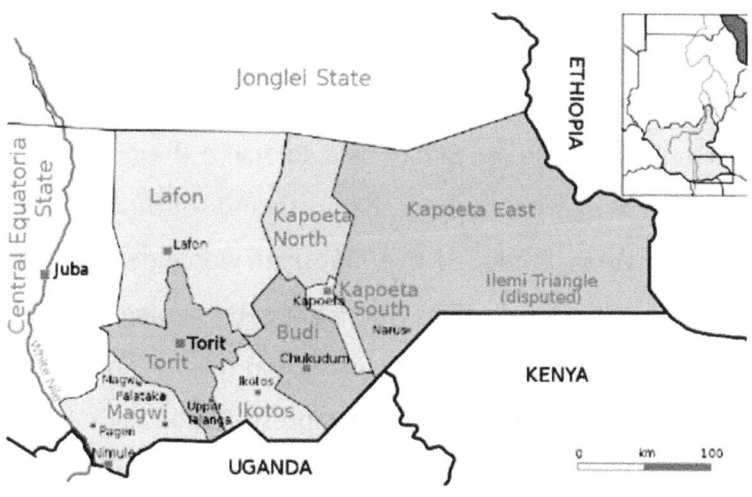

Lafon, Eastern Equitoria

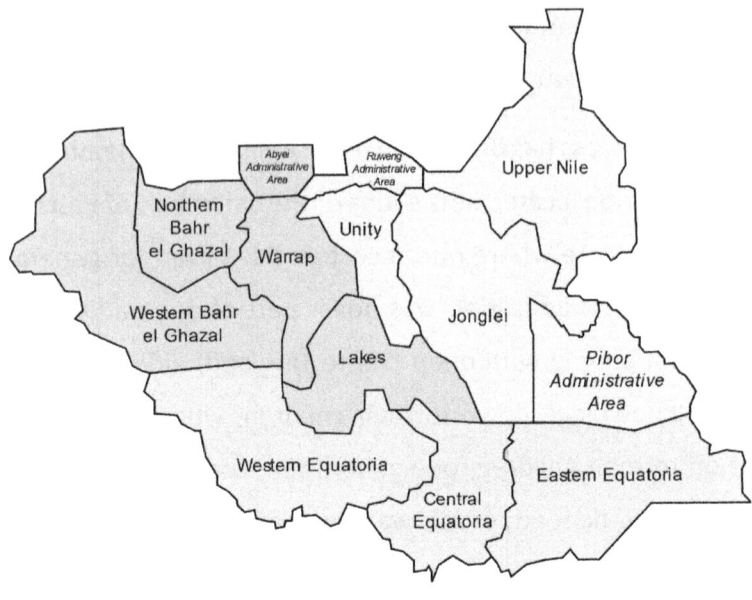

States of South Sudan

That history has forged my path. For those of you unfamiliar with my country, I will give you a quick recap. The British government ruled Sudan as a colony in the nineteenth century. They tried to unite the north and south, vastly different regions, but failed. In 1956 Sudan won independence from the UK. The conflicts that had been ongoing between the north and south over resources and religion continued. The south demanded adequate representation in Congress as well as more regional autonomy from the Islamic north. They refused. War broke out. That First Sudanese Civil War lasted until 1972 when the central government in Khartoum granted southern Sudan moderate autonomy.

During that first civil war, by pure luck—unlike countless other tribes—our Pari village in the hills was not destroyed. Our way of life did not change. In our remote tropical paradise, we remained steeped in tradition. As a result, there were few educated people in the Pari tribe compared to other ethnic groups in the region who dispersed and relocated after being attacked.

Then came the Second Sudanese Civil War. I was born in 1989, six years after it started. And that war *did* put an end to the ancient Pari way of life. Between the first and second wars, Sudan existed as one country, though the two regions have vastly different ways of life. Northern Sudan is arid, desert and semi-desert, like the Middle East. Southern Sudan is rich in natural resources, like eastern Africa, a patchwork of savannahs, prairies, rivers, lakes and jungles. While Sudan was a colony, the British developed the Arab Muslim north with infrastructure supporting modern transportation, communication, commerce—again, more like the Middle East.

The British decided to leave the south as it was—black Sudanese living in mostly rural villages like Africans in the eastern part of the continent. Northern Sudan practiced Islam, while the south practiced Christianity brought by eighteenth century missionaries. For a long time, the south had relative autonomy from the north. Villagers lived close to the land, our soil rich for farming. But there were other riches in the south as well.

Oil.

The discovery of oil fields in 1978 ended what semi-autonomy people in the south had enjoyed. Suddenly Sudan's central government in Khartoum wanted to redraw the boundary lines between north and south to include those rich oil fields.

Forcing the issue, the government also imposed Sharia law on the Christian south, among other measures mandated to break the people's will. My explanation may be simple, but it's true—oil and religion triggered the Second Sudanese Civil War.

That's where my story begins. To fight against the central government in the north with its well-equipped militia and air force, Dr. John Garang, an economist and politician in the south, started the Sudanese People's Liberation Army (SPLA), a guerilla force with little training. My father was in that army, one of many villagers captured against his will to fight when the fledgling military band needed new recruits.

The war was fought mainly in the vast agricultural heartland of the south. Government armies ravaged the countryside, brutality and cold-blooded murder forcing thousands to flee to Ethiopia, Uganda or Kenya. Most villages ended up deserted with burned huts left smoldering, fields torched, fallen soldiers remaining unburied. Villages as far as the Nuba Mountains and the Blue Nile were repeatedly attacked, civilians slaughtered, cattle stolen. It was sheer devastation throughout the south.

I was one year old when our village of Lafon was destroyed. That happened

after the SPLA came through and took my father. After capturing new recruits, they would leave the village, the government militia right behind them also coming to attack. Civilians were caught between the two. As a child, I was told that this was a revolutionary war, the liberation of southern Sudan from an oppressive central government to preserve our way of life. But what about the SPLA? What kind of liberation movement raids villages of their own people, taking men against their will as soldier recruits, shooting innocent women and children in the process?

South Sudan, 1993. Fair use image.

Instead of a personal history marking my first steps or first words, that attack on our village and the capture of my father was the milestone that began my childhood narrative, as if nothing else existed before that fateful day. But it had. The stories that my mother told me over the years as we wandered in search of a home would leave an imprint as real as that of war. Her stories made clear there was another way of life that did not include violence, bloodshed—an existence where people lived in peace with their families and died of old age surrounded by those they loved. As a child of war, I had only my mother's stories to go by. But that was enough to build a dream.

For me not only to get an education, but to finish medical school puts me in a literacy percentage with several zeros after the decimal, not only as a woman, but as a Pari woman from South Sudan. A Pari woman from South Sudan during wartime. Most people would agree mine was an impossible dream. That warring history, the backdrop to my life, underscores the unlikely chances for success. Sometimes I can hardly believe it myself—a girl born to rural village parents who grew up in a refugee camp in Kenya, a girl on her own with no money who managed to secure funding for education each step of the way for eighteen years. So much has happened. These last two decades I have kept a journal, but not in writing. In my head I have documented everything, confided in my little sister, Likali, all that I have been through, all that I have felt, including the sadness in my heart left by her death that haunts me to this day, memories breaking through when I least expect them. In medical school it had been easier to push them aside. My schedule demanded it.

Now that I am employed, the hours at the clinic are long, but the off hours are my own. There is still much reading, studying required since my residency. But the pressure feels different, leaving room for other thoughts. Like my mother and siblings still living in Kakuma Refugee Camp. How I miss them. Loneliness comes in occasional pangs as the time between visits lengthens. What would they think of me telling my life story to the world? They know so little about what really happened, how difficult it has been, what it has cost me personally. The isolation I feel working as a doctor in a village where I am related to no one is the same isolation I have felt since leaving home at twelve. That is my doing, a measure of how much energy and discipline it has taken each step of the way.

School is structured in short terms, after which everything changes. That has been my life for two decades. I cross paths with people for a few months. Then lose contact. Maybe we connect again, never for long, each of us busy chasing down a dream. That has made establishing close friendships nearly impossible. Even as a physician my life working with NGOs is based on short-term funding, at least for now, which may be the future with our hobbled government unable to pay doctors as violence continues to this day.

The friends that I *have* made along the way are now in far-flung places, our contact maintained through social media. This has been my life, a transitory existence shared with like-minded souls a few months at a time, never long enough to really know them. Or them me. It surprises me to think how little I have shared with anyone, even my mother. She has always had her hands full, keeping the family safe, fed, together. Mom and I have rarely spoken of the past. To eat, to sleep, to love and feel loved, those have been the things that absorb life's energy, for both of us. Just living has been exhausting, with little time to analyze the how or why of things. Most people in my world did not, do not welcome conversation about the suffering we experienced, the atrocities we witnessed.

All that remains tucked away inside me, only half-processed, hardships I needed to overcome without the benefit of self-reflection, as if waiting for the luxury of time. But what value can be gained talking about the intractable violence of war—women raped, young girls abducted and taken north into slavery, men snatched from their families to serve in the Resistance Army.

The strip of daylight under my door begins to fade. I slip on my sandals. Outside, the first stars appear as pale rays of sunlight splinter through the trees, refusing to yield to darkness. I walk over to the clinic office. Armed with a cup of tea, I fire up the computer. Lori has a million questions, answers to which would take forever to convey. Her first one brings an ironic smile. Yes, we must begin at the beginning.

Am I Dinka or Nuer?

I explain that I am neither. I am from the Pari tribe. South Sudan has close to ten million people, with at least sixty tribes, Dinka the largest and the one most familiar to the world beyond Sudan. That familiarity is not borne of their numbers or longevity, nor for the proud centuries-old traditions handed down from elder to youth. No, the Dinka name is known as one half of the ongoing civil war with the second largest tribe, the Nuer.

The Second Sudanese Civil War that lasted twenty-two years came to an end in 2005 when the north and south signed a peace agreement. But then our new country had its own civil war. The Dinka and Nuer have been at odds for centuries over land and cattle. When South Sudan's first president, Salva Kiir, a Dinka man, accused his vice president, Riek Machar, a Nuer man, of attempting a coup, that threw everything into chaos. Both pastoral people, cattle herders, the two tribes are not only locked in battle for land where cows no longer graze, where crops no longer flourish but for oil rights. We have had no semblance of lasting peace. African killing African is a futile effort, a hopeless battle to turn back the clock. Our land has been devastated. We continue to live with bloodshed, with deadly violence. Families cannot afford food or pay for transport. Hospitals cannot pay staff. Schools cannot pay teachers. Independent since 2011, our young country remains on the verge of economic collapse due to famine and starvation.

My shoulders slump. Do I have to go over all this background for Lori? Yes. No. South Sudan's violent history is just a Google search away. I will begin with the basics of who I am at this moment. My African name is Agwak, my clan called Pukendi. I am the oldest of five children. I pause, cringing at the next thought. How much *does* she know about South Sudan? No doubt that Google search pulled up images of Africans dressed in ethnic garb—half-naked women in ceremonial costumes, elaborate jewelry draped over their chests, which is apparently the media's favorite portrayal of rural African women.

That is not me. Most days I am wearing a simple dress beneath my lab coat. My hair is not garnished with ornaments, but pulled back behind my ears, small stone earrings the only decoration I wear besides a stethoscope around my neck, the ceremonial necklace of my adopted tribe— Doctors of Medicine. I struggle with my dual life, separated from my people not only in distance but in world view. Medicine has opened me to science that is often in conflict with the Pari belief in animism, a core tenet of my religious heritage. I am Christian, like many of my peers. Yet deep down I am bound to the culture into which I was born and hang on to that connection. I am a citizen of both worlds.

There is nothing to be gained in wondering who I might have been had everything been different. This is the life I was born to, have lived, am living, my past a part of what makes me Hellen Agwak Onyango. Yet as I approach my thirty-first year, it occurs to me that the more time that passes, the more fragile those memories become, details lost to the business of daily living. Perhaps it is time to reconcile the past.

I am a study in contrasts, with an English name, Hellen, and an African one, Agwak. I went to medical school in the metropolis of Nairobi, but practice Western medicine in a rural tribal village. There are internal contrasts too. I am happy to be here, grateful to have a job. But beneath my demeanor of contentment a huge chunk of sadness dwells in my heart from a life of too much loss. Most people find me very nice, sweet even. Yet I know what toughness it has taken to get where I am today. A soft-spoken manner belies the trauma of my childhood—a childhood stolen by war, first making me a displaced person stripped of tribal identity. Then a refugee living in a never-ending holding pattern. That was my identifying moniker for years. Refugee. Waiting for peace. Waiting to go home. Waiting to live the life my mother described in her stories.

Whatever happy ending I might have imagined at the end of medical school has been muted by the reality of a country that remains torn, a country that cannot feed or care for its people. South Sudan has failed its people. Our new identity still reflects tribal warfare. My optimism for South Sudan remains, but is fleeting, measured by the positive outcomes I have in treating my patients in this rural outpost. When I look up and see the big picture of South Sudan, I am depressed. So I keep my focus on the patients whose lives I can change in some small way that makes life better for them. That is what sustains me. And the hope for peace.

It is hard to imagine what significance my story might have. In her email Lori said that history records big events and the important leaders who made them happen. The stories of ordinary people who lived that history go untold… unless someone writes about them. I am one of those millions of people whose life unfolded unnoticed in the chaos of war. No one will know how we lived through it, other than as statistics and graphs and pie charts tracking our misery. But those do not tell our personal stories. And those stories will die with each survivor.

My life has been documented in school transcripts and completion certificates and funding applications and job resume´—my own history written in statistics. Those papers will be meaningless after I am gone. What if there is a girl out there with a dream of her own, a dream she has been told is unreachable, her future dictated by culture and tradition? *Agwak, education is the key to a better life.* What if she has no mother to tell her that she can broaden her options for the future, find a way to escape poverty, help her family, her community?

That might make my story worth writing. I have no idea what it will cost me to revisit the memories buried deep in the archives of my mind, locked away all these years. What I am certain of is that my dream has been made real, no longer in its grandiose form—to save the next generation of South Sudanese. I am only one person. There is an African proverb that says one person alone cannot clear rubble blocking the road. But she can move one pebble at a time. As a doctor I will devote whatever healing is within my capacity to build a better future for South Sudan. One patient at a time.

These thoughts are not in my email. I re-read the two paragraphs of polite responses to Lori's questions, and hit SEND.

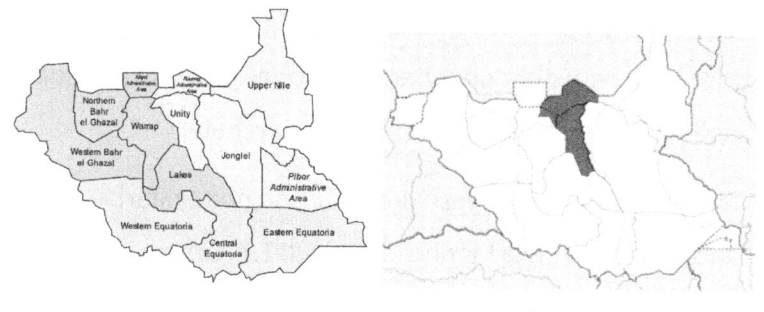

States in South Sudan   Nyal village is in Unity State

2

AN UNSTEADY PAYCHECK

Nyal, South Sudan

For a while after medical school it seemed I might never find a real job. Government funds have been gutted, so hospitals cannot pay doctors. During my search, I volunteered in pediatrics at the hospital in Juba. That was fine, the experience welcome, but I can't make a living that way. Just as things were looking dire, the International Rescue Committee officially put me on the payroll, a three-month contract, typical for NGOs with funding that is not always consistent in politically unstable regions. The IRC tells me that my contract may be extended when additional resources become available. In the meantime, I have a paycheck.

As one of the largest providers of humanitarian assistance in South Africa for decades, the IRC has been expanding the state clinic system to provide basic care in hard to reach areas. I would say Nyal qualifies. Our health here is grim. In South Sudan 61% of our people suffer from malaria, 48% are malnourished. Life expectancy is short with little access to healthcare—one doctor per 100,000 people. That explains why our median age is a little over 18 years old compared with 38 in the U.S. according to current statistics. This is a young country not only in self-governance but in demographics. Those over 65 make up only 2 % (versus 18% in the U.S.) because old people in our rural country with diabetes, heart disease, respiratory problems— treatable conditions—die with no access to doctors, let alone modern medicine.

Like everywhere else in South Sudan, Nyal's history is one of suffering. Located in Payinjiar County, it is known for the effects of extended fighting from the Second Sudanese Civil War, which led to exceptionally poor conditions, including starvation, sexual violence, destruction of roads, huts, and buildings. But as of 2015, Nyal has acted as a security centre for thousands of civilians fleeing every corner of Unity Bentiu and Eastern Upper Nile, people who came here to escape the fighting, the government militia's scorched-earth tactics committing atrocities against civilians.

Those unable to travel by boat or canoe arrived on foot, with their possessions wrapped in plastic sheets, their bundles dragging behind them on a rope. Foot travel is dangerous. South Sudan is full of swamps and rivers, which explains our fertile soil, but those bodies of water are home to poisonous snakes and crocodiles. Yet people knew they had to take that risk with a better chance of survival crossing those deadly rivers than meeting a soldier on the road.

My job here is not dangerous in that way, but the political undercurrent brings a distinct level of tension. Nyal is 100% occupied by the Nuer community, still under the rebel government of Riek Machar. As a result, no South Sudanese government agencies have operated here since the tribal conflict began in 2013. Residents of Nyal do not travel to Juba, the capital city, even during the dry season because of the presence of government forces, mostly men from the Dinka tribe. All services, including food and medical supplies, are provided by NGOs like the International Rescue Committee that employs me.

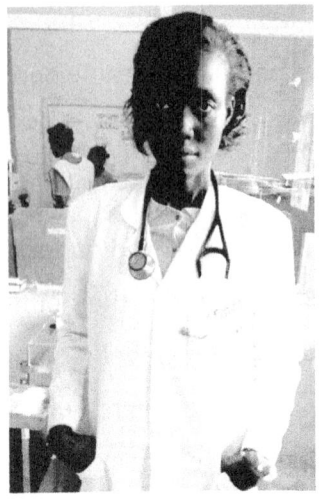

Me in medical school

My residence in Nyal.

Nyal women and children.

Nyal clinic compound.

Me with local children.

But Nyal, for all the tragedy it holds, was not the sad place that I experienced on arrival. The people, mostly women and children, were warm, hospitable, full of care, love and goodness in all aspects, precious traits in this war-torn country. The land is beautiful, typical of Sub-Saharan Africa—a mix of tropical jungles and grasslands, with groves of mango, coconut, and palm trees. During the dry months it is hot and dry. During the rainy season it is hot and wet.

Our road in the rainy season.

Nyal is a good example of the lack of access to health-care in rural South Sudan. It is incredibly isolated with no transportation between here and Juba—a distance of 353 km/219 mi—an enormous gulf between sick people in Nyal and hospital facilities in Juba. Nyal's infrastructure is inade-quate by any measure. In the rainy months, roads become impassable, especially during August and September. Relief supplies are flown in using large Ilyushin jets that land on the tiny airstrip in the dry months, by helicopter in the wet ones. I will experience both during my three-month contract, the increment by which I measure the stability of my livelihood. In the meantime, I intend to immerse myself in this job, enjoy the people, take care of my patients.

Social life will be minimal, which I am used to. Whatever contact I have in any given medical setting passes as social interaction. I will be around people all day at the clinic, while continuing to read and study on my own at night. My job entails managing the primary care clinic, including daily ward rounds for inpatients. Women and children make up the patient load. Here, as with the hospital in Juba where I volunteered, children are chronically malnourished.

Staff at the regional NGOs measure arm circumference monthly for their studies. But studies take time, and politicians are slow to act in funding humanitarian aid. In the meantime, foreign donors have become weary as the tribal war rages on, Dinka against Nuer, as millions of people suffer bloodshed and face acute food shortages. The hardest part of my work here is knowing the limits of what we can offer at the rural facility. If a patient arrives in need of critical care, chances of survival are drastically reduced.

The clinic simply is not set up for that. There is so much need for health care here in Nyal. And I am eager to do my part.

Nyal Clinic.

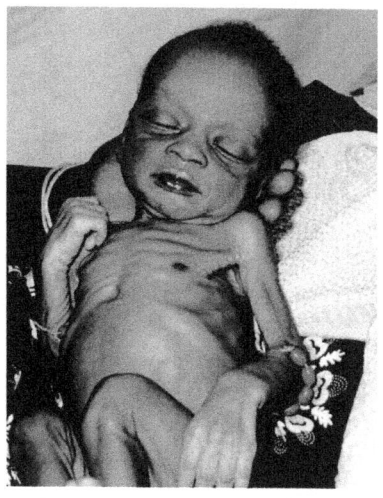

Photos courtesy of Kenneth Waxman, M.D.

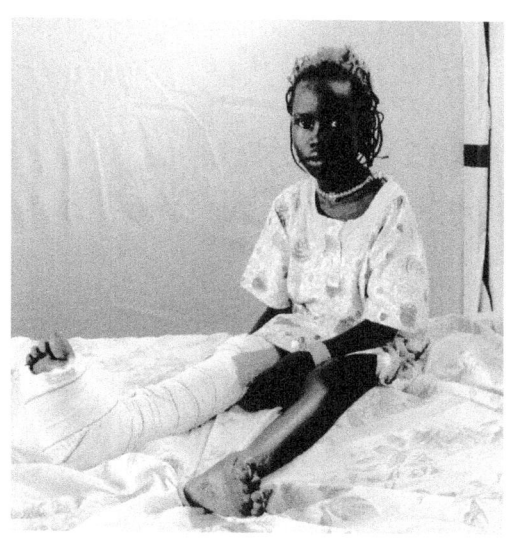

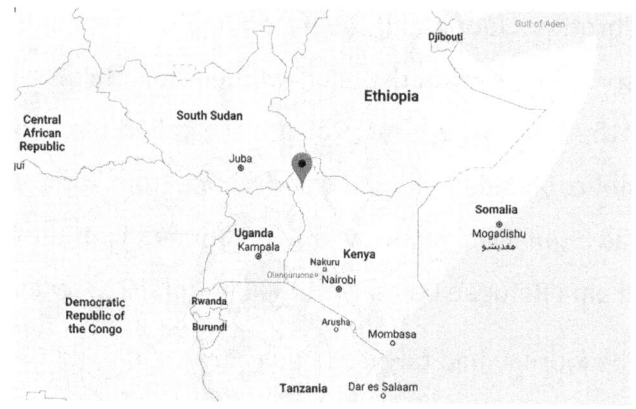

The location of the Kakuma Refugee Camp in northern Kenya.

3

THE LAND OF NOWHERE

Kakuma Refugee Camp, Kenya

If you look at the words "Kakuma Refugee Camp" on a map of Kenya, they are written in the same size font as Juba, the capital of South Sudan. Kakuma is not a city. But it is the capital of refugees. The camp was established in 1992 in northwest Kenya on the border with South Sudan to house thousands upon thousands of civilians displaced by the Second Sudanese Civil War. My mom, little sister Likali and little brother Udong and I were among the first to arrive, our sorry posse of bedraggled women and children fresh from the processing center at a place called Lokichogio a few hours outside Kakuma. The distance from Torit, where we had been living near my father stationed with the SPLA, to Kakuma Refugee Camp is 814 kilometers, 222 miles.

The journey had taken us two years.

In the large receiving room in Lokichogio, they gave us food stuffs and cooking utensils, along with bedding, our first since leaving Torit. They also gave us clothes, an over-sized blue dress with white print for me. And bread! You cannot imagine my excitement at the sight of bread. Mom said Likali and I ate so much we got diarrhea, no doubt a result of malabsorption from too much food in stomachs unaccustomed to any quantity beyond scraps.

The processing official asked my mom if we were her children. Most who arrived were not accompanied by a parent, separated from them at some point fleeing for their lives. For the first time, I wondered what might have become of me that night I got separated from Mom when our village was attacked. "Why did you leave Sudan," the official at the processing centre asked Mom. Her mouth opened slightly, but no sound came out, as if the very question were so obvious, so unnecessary that she could hardly believe the man expected an answer. As a grown woman I understand it was just government paperwork, forms needing spaces filled in with a limited choice of available responses that did not include 'tragedy.'

Public domain images.

That first night, I could not fall asleep in the processing centre, alert to unfamiliar sounds as I had been in each new place we had slept since being driven from our home. But the huge dorm was heaven—the first time in months we were able to rest, sleep at night, in sync with our circadian rhythms instead of daytime sleep and night travel when it was safer. Even in the villages where we had taken refuge along the way to Kakuma, or in the makeshift camps we formed with other groups, sleep was a luxury, danger surrounding us from animal predators and soldiers.

We stayed in the processing centre for three weeks before actually reaching Kakuma. A specific location had been assigned where we would set up housekeeping in the camp. Once we found our spot, Likali clung tight to me as we stood next to Mom, Udong—squirming in her arms—all of us staring at the surroundings, a vast expanse of dry, desolate, wind-blown plain with no living foliage in sight, save the same thorny bushes that had punctured my bare feet during months of walking.

Kakuma in the early 2000s. Public domain image.

The camp was still relatively new when we arrived in the 1995, with a mere 8,000 displaced people, most unaccompanied minors. By 2018 the barren wasteland in the northwest corner of Kenya would be home to nearly 150,000 refugees fleeing violence, famine, and suffering from disease. My family would still be among them.

Three weeks at the processing center had nourished us a bit, though with refugees pouring in every day there was never enough to eat. NGOs did the best they could, but the food supplies did not increase to meet the ever-growing number of refugees. And bandits on the road to the processing centre attacked delivery trucks, making food supplies hard to allocate for any length of time.

The bleak desert that was Kakuma—the dreamland Mom had talked about to keep us going all those months— was never meant to be a permanent housing site. Run by the UNHCR, camp sprawl was the unintended consequence of extended fighting between Dinka and Nuer after we gained independence from the north, displacing hundreds of thousands to the open countryside.

When we first came to Kakuma in 1995, like us, our neighbors arrived on foot—some having walked more than a thousand miles in search of refuge. In the early 1990s, thousands of orphaned boys had fled the carnage in villages across South Sudan, trekking to camps in Ethiopia, where they were subsequently driven out or murdered when the Ethiopian government collapsed. The world would come to know these orphaned children as "the lost boys," 20,000 strong, most of them six or seven years old, abandoned either when their parents were killed, or pled with their children to run for their lives to escape death or induction into the SPLA as child soldiers. They knew their children's chances of survival would be better crossing the crocodile-infested waters of the Gilo River into Ethiopia.

Or walking across southern Sudan in bare feet, malnourished, unprotected.

By the time the boys reached Kakuma, only half had survived.

My siblings and I were lucky to have our mother. Looking back I still cannot imagine how she kept us alive and safe all those years before we reached Kakuma. Other than those times when we settled in peaceful villages for a few weeks or months, we had been in danger either from starvation or murder, like everyone else in the camp—displaced by war, an entire way of life vanishing overnight.

People at both the processing centre in Lokichogio and the camp itself talked about going to America. Even refugees with nothing but the clothes on their back and a water gourd assumed the stay in Kakuma would be short term. Their dreams of relocating to the U.S. were not without substance. In the 1980s and '90s, America had been accepting a limited number of refugees from Africa, those who fled to neighboring countries or had stayed in their own, displaced by war or famine. Orphaned children could be sponsored in the United States through religious organizations and other volunteer groups who matched them with willing families. Likali and John Udong and I were not orphaned. Nor did we have a desire to relocate anywhere but home. How could we have known that this swath of barren dust wedged between two dry rivers would become that place?

Kakuma's inhospitable terrain was aptly named. In Swahili, *Kakuma* means 'nowhere.' If anyplace described a Land of Nowhere, it was Kakuma. As Mom kept reminding us, the place may not have been the lush savannah of our tribal Lafon, but Kakuma had one thing going for it that no other place we had been in five years had—safety. Mom had been consumed with anxiety protecting us during years of displacement. In the big picture, staying alive was the overriding goal that made our acquaintance with venomous spiders, snakes, scorpions and malaria-carrying mosquitoes nothing more than a daily nuisance. Mom talked about living in safety the way others talked about independence for southern Sudan, both subjects conveyed in reverent tones alluding to a better future. For us, that future meant no more planes dropping bombs during the day, like fire from the sky, and no marauding soldiers attacking in the dead of night. For the first time in our short lives, Likali, Udong and I would be able to play freely in Kakuma.

That first day I did not see the beauty of such freedom. I did not see beauty at all. Even as a six-year-old the sight of the place shocked me. Life in the bushes had been brutal—never-ending hunger, scrounging for edible berries or small rodents—our decimated bodies in a constant state of dehydration. But there had been shade, deep green foliage in those bushes that allowed us to escape from heat as we walked endless miles. There was no shade in Kakuma, no escape from the heat, no edible berries to stave off hunger.

None of that mattered. My father would find us when the fighting ended and take us back to our homeland, our village in Lafon. A few months in Kakuma would be tolerable I supposed. The important thing was that we were together. And had a home at last.

The morning sun in Nyal woke me. At the clinic by eight o'clock, I quickly scanned email looking for a response from Lori before starting rounds. Our eleven-hour time difference had narrowed overnight. Her enthusiasm was palpable judging by the first barrage of questions: How did I get to Kakuma? Who was I with? What was the camp like? I leaned back with a smile. The clinic was full. Lori's questions would have to wait. I closed the computer and began rounds.

The next time I glanced outside the sun was high, afternoon heat pulsing through the clinic walls. I welcomed the opportunity to sit down to chart on my patients—pregnant women with pre-eclampsia, making them high risk for delivery—children with malaria needing intravenous rehydration, elderly with hypertension. The slate of differential diagnoses had a wide range, the clinic a lifeline for villagers with myriad conditions. Activity on the ward had slowed to a lull by late afternoon. I grabbed a cup of tea and headed for the shady bench outside.

Lori's questions about my past may not have been answered in writing yet, but simply reading them triggered an avalanche of memories, almost a reflex response. A lifetime had passed since I had taken the first step that got me to where I was, sitting under a shady tree as the resident physician in the Nyal clinic. I stared into the distance. Had I known at the outset the number of obstacles that lay before me, how big and seemingly hopeless to master, would I have taken that first step? I smiled. Of course I would have. As a girl of twelve there was no way to see beyond my childhood dream. Ignorance nurtured courage.

Money. That has always been the biggest obstacle. That was my biggest conflict, one that I carried every single step of the way. The other obstacles were internal—self-doubt, loneliness, the pressure to succeed with someone else financing my way forward. Childhood dreams rarely include financial concerns. That's what makes them dreams. You see the end, and if it is powerful enough, the means are just a detail to address along the way. In medical school I used to think that once I became a doctor, money worries would evaporate with a steady paycheck. The job market was too far in the future to worry about. My hands were full scrambling for funding to stay in school. It had never occurred to me that with a government still unable to pay salaries, NGOs would be my employers for the foreseeable future. The never-ending anxiety over financial security would not be the reward for having achieved my dream. That particular curse would shadow me for who knew how long until we found real peace and stability in South Sudan.

As I sipped tea, memories from my past mixed with thoughts about the present, fast-forwarding and rewinding in a collage of scenes. My memories are secondhand stories overheard in conversations between my mother and my aunt on those rare occasions when they spoke about the past in waves of nostalgia rather than remorse. The morning my father was abducted by the SPLA, he had been out in the fields, as he was most mornings as a farmer. I was a toddler, Likali not yet born. This fleeting thought of my father brings a warm rush. I try to picture him. The contours of his face have faded, his eyes mere shapes without expression. How frustrating that I cannot pull up his image from some database in my mind. One precious photograph—that is all I have by which to remember him. I feel tears build, but they do not fall. In my culture tears are reserved for moments of extreme anguish. I have cried those very real tears.

But I have learned what I suspect all of us who survived know—having lived with unendurable loss, the constant fear for our lives, our bodies near-starvation, the weight of despair—whatever it was we had felt—somehow we understood that if everyone were to express their feelings, the collective sorrow would bring us to our knees. In a silent pact it was understood that each of us must carry her burden alone to spare others, those among us whose might be heavier. And so I called my un-cried tears 'heart tears' that flowed in torrents of sadness unleashed by a random memory that would catch me off guard—a child whose laugh sounded like Likali's, the smell of fresh sorghum. I cannot control these flashes of memory, nor can I express them, so fleeting the pang, so tender the feelings they bring. But for a moment I am transported backward in time.

The memory of that morning as it has been told to me reminds me that it would be the last time I saw my father come in from his chores, my mother there with his breakfast. It would be later that very night that SPLA soldiers invaded our house, forcibly removing my father to join their ranks. He resisted, explaining that he had responsibilities—a wife and child, a farm, cattle. "Come now," they demanded, "or we kill you in front of your wife." What must that moment have been like for my parents, their farewell a quick tormented glance to convey their feelings for each other, the joy of our being a family with a good life, the despair of that life now resting in the hands of rebel soldiers.

Mom said no one in our remote village of Lafon had known the movements of the SPLA, much less suspect they might raid our village one day. It was only later that we learned the liberation army had been formed as a guerrilla movement in

1983 against the central government when it tried to take control of the south, which meant oil. The fledgling rebel army showed the north they meant business, blocking government projects—including the pumping of oil from the fields.

In Khartoum, the government might not have worried too much about this grass roots ragtag army, except that by this time the Ethiopian government had provided military training and weapons for it based on their own reasons for stopping the long reach of the central government in Sudan. My parents along with everyone else knew nothing of this growing tension between the north and south. There had been rumors about it, but no one knew for sure what took place beyond the remote hills of our paradise in Lafon.

But the more victories the guerrillas scored, the more the central government worried. The final straw had been an unimaginable strike by the rebel army. Guerrillas had captured a small town in Ethiopia, hundreds of miles from Sudan's capital in Khartoum, taking control of the dam that provided its electricity. It turned out the ragtag army was more of a threat than the government thought. And it would have to be conquered. After that it was all-out war.

To make matters worse, dissent that had been brewing in the SPLA finally broke the liberation army into opposing factions. Rather than fighting for oil and religious freedom, the new dissidents who followed Dr. John Garang demanded secession from Sudan—an independent South Sudan.

Followers or Riek Machar wanted autonomy for the south but remain a single secular country of Sudan.

The end result of all this chaos was that not only was the government in Khartoum in the north fighting the SPLA in every village in the south, but the two warring SPLA factions in the south were fighting each other for control. Civilians were caught in the crossfire, attacked by one army often followed by the other, village men captured by the SPLA to fill the ranks as untrained rebel soldiers fell under the weapons of modern warfare used by the north. The SPLA raided villages not only for men, like my father, but boys as young as twelve were captured, given guns, forced to fight or die.

Our Pari tribes' six villages in Lafon became a flashpoint. It turns out our paradise on Lipul Hill (Jebel Lafon) was an ideal location, a strategic crossroads connecting not only Eastern Equitoria and Upper Nile-Gambella, but also Pibor, Bor, Kapoeta, Torit, Mongalla and Juba towns. The government was desperate to control this area. The SPLA stood in its way. And the only way the rebel army could hold firm against the government was to build its numbers with new recruits.

The night of my father's capture ended his career as a farmer. Without men to tend the crops, our fields went fallow. Cattle were stolen or killed. Our huts were burned to ashes by the government militia who followed behind the SPLA. Mom and I had left before that. Along with other women, children and elderly, we gathered what food, cooking pots and clothes we could, setting out on foot. At first no one knew where to go with reports of neighboring villages under attack. Then came news that the SPLA had set up its headquarters in the town of Torit. That would be where my father was stationed. And so we headed southeast to Torit town.

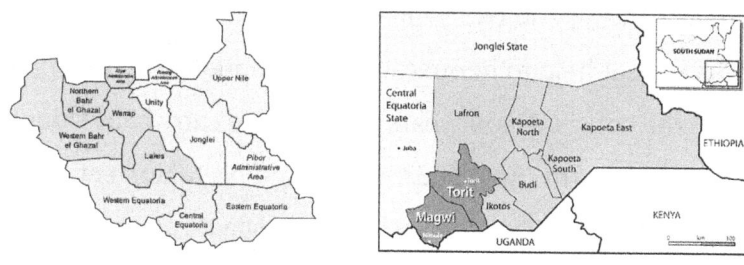

Lafon is in Eastern Equitoria Eastern Equitoria

Our little band of women, children, and disabled men unwanted by the army walked for days on end in the Sudanese heat. To avoid soldiers from either side we traveled at night, which also helped us cope with the heat. How long it took us, I do not know. Mom said that when we reached the outskirts of Torit, our group set up a makeshift camp and settled into some semblance of a routine, searching for food and carrying water from the nearest bor hole, which made us unwelcome tenants in Torit.

As long as Mom was close enough that my father could visit, she was content to wait out the war. But the threat of attack by the government militia was a constant fear. Oblivious to our situation, I played with the other kids, and lived like any other child. Dad visited when he could.

It was in Torit that I became a big sister. Likali was born that first year, and two years later John Udong. Mom said I was a great help to her because all I wanted to do was play with the babies. At four years old, I liked to carry baby Udong around, my arms wrapped tight around his torso, feet dragging in the dirt. Occasionally he would slip through my arms and roll to the ground with a giggle. Mom would give me a sidelong glance as she dusted him off and sat him next to where she cooked on the stove outside. She never got mad at me. In fact, as I recall, it was on those occasions that she smiled—in spite of my dropping Udong in the dirt—no doubt our laughter a welcome salve for the soundtrack of gunfire in the background.

Fair Use image.

Torit is where we stayed the longest. My father was off fighting for long stretches sometimes, which made Mom unhappy. Much of daily life was consumed with finding food for that day, just staying alive. Sometimes at night Mom would talk to me about our Pari tribe in Lafon, about a life with plentiful food. Farmers in our paradise cultivated sorghum for use as grain or syrup, cowpeas, greengrams, pumpkin, okra, sesame and tobacco. Pari farmers had plenty of work all year round. My father loved working the land more than tending cattle and sheep that grazed on our hillsides. But livestock were special for my people. Boys as young as six began learning to watch over cattle.

Livestock connected us not only to each other, neighbor to neighbor in this world, but also connected us to the world of our gods. We used livestock in trade, as we did our produce. A man's wealth was determined by the number of cattle he owned. We were not wealthy, but my father provided for us and shared with our neighbors. In the dry season my father hunted and fished in the two rivers, the Hoss and Hinyetti. There was never a shortage of dried and smoked fish, as well as edible plants. Mom would recount stories of these riches when we were so hungry walking the countryside. You would be hard pressed to find a healthier diet than that of our Pari tribe.

But farming, fishing and hunting need men.

Photo courtesy of Kenneth Waxman, M.D.

Fair use image.

My daydream bubble burst as I sat with my tea in the shade. The day shift was ready to leave the clinic. The night shift would be taking over after getting report for the smooth transition of patient care. I scrunched my neck. If only I could transcribe my thoughts into writing. It is clear to me that to write my story it must be more than a recitation of facts, a safe, clean intellectual exercise. Things will come up, as they have today. But I am also increasingly aware that the only way we can survive our own memories is to shape them into a story, a story that makes sense out of events that are inexplicable.

I have seen the horrors that humans can inflict on one another. But I have also witnessed acts of tenderness and kindness and sacrifice in the worst imaginable circumstances. There have been times when everything seemed hopeless, human dignity lost to savagery. I was beginning to see that the story of my life was a history of the choices I made in the daily act of surviving. The one constant in my thirty years on this earth has been the conviction that given the freedom to live as a healer, to love my family, believe in my God, I would serve South Sudan, and restore some of the human dignity to those who suffered so much from this war, who suffer still.

4

IN SEARCH OF SHELTER
Southern Sudan: Torit to Kapoeta

It was a bright Sunday morning, the clinic quiet. Times like these were a good opportunity to finish up loose ends from a busy week. The sound of men shouting outside drew my attention, a not-unwelcome interruption from reading *South Sudan Guidelines on Management of Common Diseases*. It might as well have been a book on life-threatening illnesses. In rural South Sudan, common conditions left without treatment often had the same outcome. I stuck a bookmark in place and stepped outside.

My assistant, Theresa, off work on a Sunday, had also come out to investigate the commotion on the road in front of the clinic. Together we watched the scene unfold. Half a dozen men stood knee-deep in a sea of mud from the previous nights' rain. A flatbed lorry was stuck in the middle of the road, its wheels on one side buried to their rims. The driver grimaced as he leaned out the window, his body at an awkward angle with the pitch of the truck. Locals had attached ropes to the opposite

side and the front bumper. Shouting to the driver to go ahead and rev the engine, they gave a collective grunt trying to get the vehicle back on all fours.

Outside the clinic in Nyal. Below, I am in the center.

As the engine roared, the buried wheels, unable to gain traction, spun stubbornly in place, flinging mud like machine gun fire at the men pulling the rope.

The sound of men yelling triggered memories of another truck, another time—the end of our stay in Torit. It had been hot then, not wet. Government forces made a surprise attack of the SPLA headquarters, and in its path, the make-shift settlements on the outskirts. It was all we could do to gather what we could of our belongings. Once again, we ran for our lives—only this time besides me and Mom there was Likali, a toddler, and the baby, Udong.

I don't remember how long we walked. I just remember walking in the dark, scrounging for food in the bushes, then walking again, not stopping to sleep until daybreak. I did my best to pull my sister along by the hand. When she could no longer keep up, I carried her as far as my four-year-old emaciated body could manage. Then we would stop to rest, though Mom was desperate to stay with the others as a group for protection.

Even had the militia not attacked our little settlement in Torit, we would have left. By then, life had become unsustainable with increasingly frequent attacks by armed groups along roads leading in and out of town, including attacks on NGO vehicles, preventing vital food and other goods from getting through. All of us were near starvation, and the fighting was only getting worse. The attack was the final impetus. As we prepared for bed one night, gunshots rang out in the distance. Mom told me to say my prayers and go to bed. Outside our hut she gathered with the other women to confer. In South Sudan on a moonless night, it is so dark you can stand two feet away talking to someone and not see her face. That was the kind of night this was.

Mom rushed back inside, her voice filled with tension. Dress quickly, she said. But there was no time. Gunshots cracked through the darkness, close to us. Mom scooped up the baby, slung him into the swaddling cloth around her neck, then grabbed my hand in one of hers, Likali's in the other. Outside our hut we stood motionless in the dark. It was mayhem, everyone screaming, running in different directions, the whole village fleeing, burning huts throwing flashes of light on the horrific scene. I didn't understand what was happening.

Then I saw fear on people's faces as they raced by, adults in panic, mothers hanging on to their children, gunshots coming closer as we stood in terror. Mom broke into a run, Likali and I in tow, the baby jostling safely against Mom's chest. The next moment I stopped, shocked by the scene before me. Two friends I had played with that very evening lay on the ground, motionless, blood pooling around them. Everything stopped. I heard nothing but the pounding of my heart, my inert body a blockade forcing others to go around me on either side, knocking my shoulders as they passed.

Stunned, I watched as neighbors sidestepped my playmates to avoid trampling their crumpled bodies. At first, I thought I was dreaming. Then I thought I might die, too. So many people, running, running in different directions. Mom was nowhere in sight. I gasped, scanning the mayhem for her orange dress. I screamed. "Mom!" nothing. I yelled again, my voice lost in the cacophony, sheer pandemonium in the mass exodus.

Someone grabbed me by the arm. From out of nowhere our neighbor yanked me alongside her. It was Imoya, a teenage girl who sometimes looked after us younger ones when our mothers went to fetch water at the river. She was yelling something to me, pulling me along as she ran. I finally gathered my wits. Imoya slid her hand down my arm, grasping my hand tight. We ran through the gruesome slaughter—neighbors motionless on the ground, huts on fire, black smoke dulling the bright orange flames, babies crying, goats bleating—a nightmare, sights and sounds too sickening to comprehend. "Faster, Agwak," Imoya beckoned me.

I held on tight to her as we sprinted through the maze dodging bullets. A neighbor lady running with her children in the opposite direction nearly collided into us. Stunned to see us going the other way, she reversed course. I wanted to ask her if she had seen my mom. There was no way she would have heard me in the melee. My body was leaden, each step weighed down with fear. What if Mom was running in the other direction too? The further we got from the burning huts, the darker it was, too dark to see soldiers, but not too dark to hear their guns, or the screams of those around us getting shot, falling down. As young as I was, I can still remember the crack of gunfire, the grisly feel of stepping in pools of blood with my bare feet, dead neighbors all around me. I thought I might faint and be left for dead. But Imoya kept hold of me.

We ran and ran further into the bushes. Out of breath, we would stop to listen. But the gunfire always sounded close. And so without words or signals or a plan, onward we went, deeper and deeper into the bushes. One of the neighbor kids, a four-year-old boy, collapsed in exhaustion in front of us. He lay on the ground crying. Where was his mother? Were we going to leave him there? Suddenly his mother appeared. In one swift motion, she slung him over her shoulder and kept running. The next time we stopped the gunfire sounded farther away. Our pace slowed, but we did not stop moving until first light. Small groups of villagers passed us, some followed behind. Not one of them was wearing an orange dress.

For two days we followed the mothers, children and old men through the bushes in search of safety. Everything green had a thorn. My feet were raw, legs scratched, my thin nightgown offering little protection. Everything hurt, my misery compounded by the fact that I had no idea where my mother was. I began to wonder if there would ever be enough water to quench my thirst. We had no water gourds with us, no time to grab them. At first light we stopped moving, then scattered in search of berries, the only food we could find, staying in sight of each other.

The morning sun beat down as we tried to sleep, but with no bedding, no barrier between me and the snakes and mosquitos and spiders, it was impossible. I dozed on and off, my eyes half open. In the bushes, even in daylight, everything is alive. My heart raced listening to animal sounds in the distance, nearby waterholes an early morning wildlife destination. Their primordial communication warned other species to steer clear of marked territory. Including us. I managed to doze off. At one point I opened my eyes to a huge ugly scorpion with menacing pincers moving toward me. I jumped up, thrashing at the ground. It was all Imoya could do to quiet me so I would not wake the others. That was the end of sleep for me. Wide awake, I sat next to Imoya, scanning the group. Every day more people joined us, all of us confused as to where we were going or when we might find shelter. Or food and water. None of that would have mattered had I only been with my mom.

I convinced myself that she and Likali and Udong had gone in the other direction. I wanted to cry, but in my dehydrated state, only dry sobs emerged. At dawn on the third day we prepared to hunker down in the bushes to sleep. I glanced up to make sure Imoya was near me as she cleared our sleeping area. Other children had gravitated toward her as well, the village babysitter even in our displacement. I figured since she had been separated from her mom, maybe she needed me as much as I needed her. Except she was almost an adult, I was only four. But I had always felt older, more adult than child. As we settled down to sleep, sunlight hitting us like shards of glass with its heat, I looked up to see a small group settling not far from us, across the road under an Acacia tree. Bright orange swirled across my visual field for a split second.

Was I imagining it? Tiptoeing to the road, I softly called out, praying no soldiers were within earshot. The woman did not turn around. I called again. This time she did. Mom. Light as the wind, I ran as fast as my legs would go. The orange dress grew bigger and bigger. Likali burst toward me like a meteor, both of us smashing into each other with such force that we stumbled backward. Then Mom reached me, the three of us locked in a group hug so tight I thought my heart might pop out of my chest. Holding Likali in one hand and me with the other, Mom spoke with Imoya very quickly before we scurried to her group and collapsed in a heap, the three of us right next to where Udong slept like the baby he was. I had never known such joy. Neither scorpions nor snakes nor mosquitos could keep me from the deep sleep that pulled me under while I lay in my mother's arms that night. I vowed that never again would I be separated from my family.

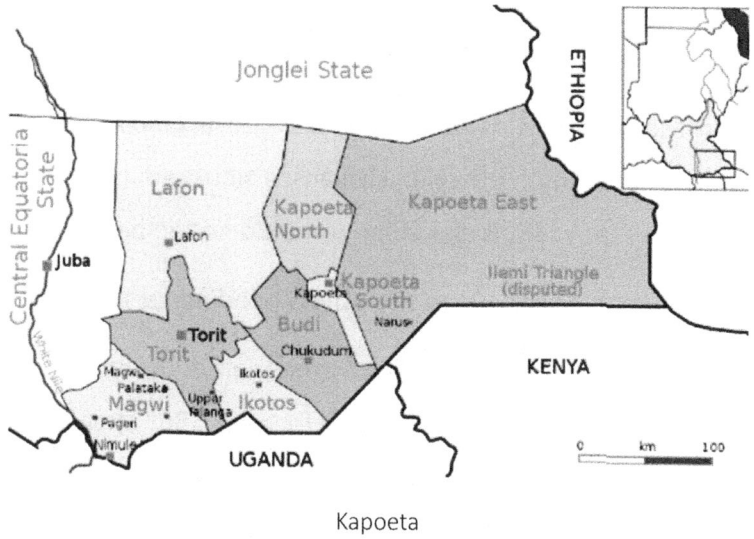

Kapoeta

The next night we finally reached a neighboring village. They took us in, fed us, gave us water. But we could not stay. Rumor had it that soldiers were on their way. It mattered little whether they were government militia or the rebel army. Civilians were collateral damage. But for one night we were fed, hydrated. The next morning our group disbanded. Some people had family in Juba a few hundred kilometers away and would take that route. Others would head for the border of Uganda. The rest were headed for Kapoeta Town.

Mom was hesitant about joining the exodus to Kapoeta. It was supposedly a sanctuary from fighting where food was available from neighboring areas not occupied by soldiers.

But Mom wanted to stay closer to Torit, convinced that my dad would return after the fighting stopped. When an elder told Mom he had news of near-total devastation in Torit, that It was uninhabitable, civilians ambushed by armed groups as they left, it was clear we could not go back.

Reluctantly, we joined the others heading for Kapoeta.

The Torit - Kapoeta Road was the main route. If we followed it, we would make our way to safety. But apparently the random bandits we had seen from a distance while hiding in the bushes were less a threat than the armed ones staked out along the main road. As we headed off toward Kapoeta, all eyes were alert for thieves lying in wait. As I had with Imoya, we traveled by night, slept in the bushes by day, and scrounged for anything edible. The terrain was hilly. Even walking at night was hard with no food to sustain us as we dragged ourselves from one village to the next in search of shelter.

When we found it, a small village along the way, we would stay for several days. Sometimes a few weeks. There was no way to know where we were exactly, where the next village was, or how long we could stay in the current one before dwindling resources or imminent attack forced us out. The funny thing about being displaced is that there is *no place* for you. However nice the villagers who took us in, they too were struggling to survive. And so we got used to being transients, resting just long enough to move on.

As we neared the Kapoeta South County border, I could sense excitement growing in Mom and the other women. At last, a place where we could stop for a while. Kapoeta Town was a pastoral community like Lafon with herds of cattle and goats grazing nearby. Best of all the town had ten boreholes, which meant more functional taps than there had been in Torit. There we had run out of water, the boreholes stretched beyond capacity by the influx of soldiers and the families who followed them. Mom had spent hours each day bringing water in pails from the river. There was no way we could have stayed in Torit, even had the fighting stopped.

Water in Kapoeta Town was rationed, but accessible. Like food and other goods, fuel came by road from Uganda. But as with everything that gets neglected by war, and the poverty it brings, lack of maintenance had caused the boreholes to break down, with no way to dig new ones. We did not stay long in Kapoeta. But not because of a water shortage. Three months after setting up housekeeping, Sudan government forces headed toward us. That was all the news we needed to move on. We later heard that for two days Kapoeta was bombarded as militia moved in and took control, turning it into a ghost town like every other place they had attacked—raping, killing, burning, plundering their way across South Sudan, destroying all communities suspected of supporting the SPLA. People of Kapoeta scattered. As we had in Torit, Mom, Likali, Udong and I had gotten out just in time.

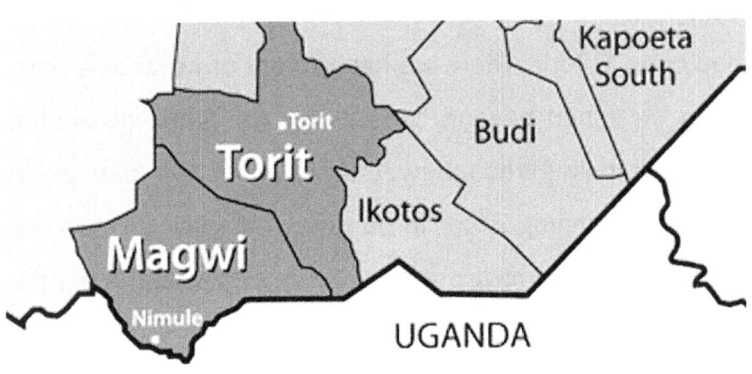

5

A TASTE OF PARADISE

Nimule, South Sudan

As the months rolled by, Udong learned to walk and talk, Likali got bigger, and I grew too. Talk of the Kakuma Refugee Camp in Kenya gathered steam after we left Kapoeta Town. Food, water and the presence of NGOs made the camp sound attractive. Mom was not ready to give up the idea of returning to Torit and finding my father once the fighting let up. So instead of heading to Kakuma to the east of us in Kenya, my cousin Abraham joined us—me, Mom, Likali, Udong and a few others as we made our way to a place called Nimule near the border with Uganda. We would still be in southern Sudan. Mom said that was better than going to Kakuma. She was not sure if we would need to pay for a visa to get into Kenya, at which point we would have been turned away. All kinds of rumors circulated in this time of uncertainty with little reliable information. Driven by anxiety, much of the news was inaccurate.

And so late one night we bade goodbye to those heading east to Kakuma and began walking south. It was 602 km/374 miles from Kapoeta to Nimule. The other villages and towns we had stayed in were near Kapoeta. Nimule was a world away. Mom said such a distant place is what made it desirable. We would be safe there, far from the fighting. The wildlife preserve established under British rule offered a natural buffer zone to the rest of southern Sudan. But to get there, basically, we had to retrace our footsteps in the direction of Torit, then continue south toward Uganda until we reached Nimule. Kapoeta had offered a resting place long enough that we began the long, arduous journey feeling strong.

Like our trek from Torit to Kapoeta, the terrain was hilly from Torit to Nimule. It was not as hard to walk through with wide grasslands, but food was scarce. Still too little to walk much on their own, Abraham carried either Likali or Udong most of the time. It felt good to have him with us. He and Mom traded off. For the first time, all I carried was my water gourd. The challenge still was to travel on foot by night, staying out of sight of the armed groups using the same main roads during the day.

At night, it was a different world, the inhabitants showing their faces. Not spiders and snakes and scorpions, though they were there too. Wildlife wandered freely along the road crossing the bushes—zebras, bushbuck, warthogs, baboons, and an occasional jackal. I had never seen such beautiful country as the one we walked between Kapoeta and Nimule. Even though we were soaked to the bone most of the time. When we left Kapoeta the rainy season had just begun.

We knew little about the place we were headed, and how the roads would be. It was our good fortune that Nimule was accessible even during the wet months, high plains less prone to flooding. We did not mind being soaked to the skin. It helped with the heat. And the further away we got from Kapoeta the safer we felt, deep in the south of Sudan, awed by its beauty.

As it had in Kapoeta, and in Torit, and in all the villages where we stopped in between, life in Nimule moved in stop-and-start rhythm according to the immediacy of threat. That threat did not come for two years. In the meantime we lived in peace with some feeling of stability in our hideaway paradise, knowing it was only a matter of time before government forces pushed south.

That day finally came.

Nimule, South Sudan. Fair use images.

By then I was six years old, accustomed to leaving what had become a series of temporary homes. As long as my family was together, our location did not matter much to me. In Nimule, just as it had in Kapoeta, talk of the refugee camp in Kenya circulated among us, but not with the same urgency as it had in less protected towns. I had no idea what a refugee was exactly, how it was different from a regular person, but I knew that I was one. The camp part of 'refugee camp' I took to mean like the ones we had made on the outskirts of Torit, and in Kapoeta.

Mom had never stopped hoping we could return there to Torit and reunite with my dad. It was not just because we had no visa to enter Kenya that she had rejected Kakuma. In Kenya the distance between my parents would be greater than ever. Mom clung to her hope the way I would later cling to mine, never losing sight of the end goal. But something happened that quashed her hope of returning to Torit.

After leaving Nimule, we passed through a place called New Cush in the Lotukei Mountains. Mom found out it was the new headquarters of the SPLA, a training camp for Special Forces. When she asked one of the soldiers about my father, I could see the flicker of hope in her eyes. But my father was not there. And no one could tell us where he was.

By default, we kept walking east, away from the fighting, away from my father toward Kenya. Our small band of women and children stopped for a few days here, a few days there, in one village after another, evicted along with the locals when reports reached us of enemy soldiers on their way. Whether or not those reports were true had become a moot point. The towns and villages behind us had been wiped out. Mom had run out of options. There was only one place left.

Kakuma.

And so we kept moving east toward southern Sudan's border with Kenya in search of the refugee camp that would become our home. I had never been outside of Eastern Equitoria, our state, and had no concept of the size of it, nor of southern Sudan. Nimule on the border with Uganda had been a long way from Kapoeta, a few hundred miles. Even so, we covered the distance in a matter of months. From that experience I concluded southern Sudan was not so big.

Our journey from Nimule to Kakuma proved me wrong. For weeks, months, we traveled southern Sudan on foot, citizens of Inbetweendom, a purgatory straddling the known and the unknown. Likali and Udong had to be carried most of the time, like the other children whose small bodies had been undermined by malnutrition. Kenya was another planet. My mother assured us that our new home would be a good place, not as good as Nimule perhaps, but much better compared with the miserable one in Torit. It turns out that proximity to my father had been the only good thing about Torit.

Kapoeta had been better than Torit, and Nimule better than Kapoeta. Mom said Kakuma would be the best place yet. Safe from the war, we would be able to stay there indefinitely. Which meant until my father came to take us back to Lafon, the place where my mom had been happy. Of course, that life was gone, ending the night our village was destroyed and we fled for our lives. My mother knew that. But returning to our village in Lafon was the dream that kept her going all those months as she got her children safely across southern Sudan on foot.

Travel was brutal. We went days without anything to eat. My stomach gnawed, grinding in misery against itself finding nothing to digest. Nuts and berries and edible plants became our staples. When we were lucky, some of the women or older kids would catch a rat or two and roast it. Even for our small posse, it took a lot of rodents to make a meager meal, and certainly not enough to replenish the nutrients we burned plodding on foot, women and children as young as two, forging a path to this place called Kakuma.

Mom's mood became subdued once she learned we could not rejoin my father in Torit. I was sad too. But like Mom, I kept it inside. Even at six, I knew Mom was worried about him. She would fervently remind us that we would see him once the fighting ended. But the fighting did not end. And the walking did not stop. Exhaustion became my normal state. At night in single file behind Mom, half asleep, eyes closed, I would clutch her skirt, my feet moving in rhythm with hers, the synchrony of survival keeping us in lock step. In moments when I wanted to give up, she would thwart despair, pointing in the moonlight, 'See that Acacia tree in the distance? Just get that far, Agwak, then we will rest.'

We did rest, but never long enough. The cover of night would give way to daybreak, and on we would go, half asleep, hungry. Always hungry. I don't remember how many nights we walked. Time didn't exist as days and nights—a twenty-four-hour cycle—but as one long continuous corridor of misery, with nothing behind or in front of us. The bottom of my feet had been toughened by the walk from Torit to Kapoeta, and Kapoeta to Nimule. But two years of living in Nimule had made them vulnerable again to the pebbles and thorns. Whatever anxiety I had about this new place called Kakuma had been subsumed by physical depletion and mental exhaustion. Had I come face-to-face with a ferocious lion I might have welcomed it as merciful deliverance.

But, no, I could not succumb to my deteriorating body, or my waning spirit. I was brave, Mom said. She needed me to be a big girl. She also needed to believe she could protect me, even though we both knew that was impossible in the case of a lion, or a marauding soldier. Like any child that age, I believed my mother was all-knowing, all-powerful, that whatever bad there was in the world, she would protect me from it. When I played with friends in Torit or Kapoeta, Mom dug ditches for us to jump into when fire fell from the sky. On the open road, the untamed grasslands and prairies and mountains we were crossing, the only protection was our own wits. And luck.

I now realize that this quiet but significant revelation that my mother could not protect me marked the end of my childhood. Even if my father had appeared on the road to Kakuma and whisked us back to our village that very moment, it had become clear to me that never again would I be a carefree child. At six years old, I had already seen death, unimaginable suffering and brutality, lived with constant fear for my life, chronic hunger, and had wandered the earth in search of safety. Although my young mind could neither process nor articulate this new awareness, on some deeper level I was much older than my chronological age from exposure to suffering no child should experience or witness. My mom had been able to bear all that she had been through, seen. On that endless journey to Kakuma, I vowed that I would be like her. I would put one foot in front of the other. And hold on to hope beyond all reasonable expectation.

In that random moment on an unconscious level, Mom became my role model for coping. At the time of course, this was all a vague understanding, one which took years to crystallize. I yielded to Mom's comfort during those long months in the bushes when sleep evaded me in the hot sun on an empty stomach. She would curl her body around me, stroke my hair and whisper that soon we would get to the refugee camp. Just knowing we had a destination calmed me. And one day soon we would see my father. That was her mantra, repeated often. Many nights it was the last thing I heard before drifting off, Mom wrapped around me like a protective cacoon, Likali tucked close, her face next to mine.

6

THE LONGEST WALK

Somewhere in Sudan

The journey to Kakuma took forever. Already a thin girl, my emaciated body made me look even younger. But I was strong. At only three, Likali could hold her own for a long time, but eventually she would literally fall asleep walking. Then I would carry her piggyback style. The pressure of her body against mine made me feel stronger, as if our combined strength had doubled. Besides, my sister

was a lightweight, made even lighter by her sweet dis-
position. Likali was a bright presence in our midst, her
giggle boosting our spirits. And how we all needed that
boost.

Some days I was convinced that life was passing me
by, that I would never be like other girls who had a real
home, instead walking endlessly, stuck on a treadmill going
nowhere. Maybe we had been walking in circles. How would
we know? One morning I got the answer. The sun had risen
quickly with no trees to block its light, ending our nocturnal
trek. Adults dropped their bags holding whatever belongings they had, usually a cup or bowl, a few nuts, a cloth for
wrapping their faces against mosquitoes.

A hush fell over the group. A low hum purred somewhere
in the distance. No one breathed. A vehicle was approach-
ing. A truck. The sound got louder. My mother walked back
to the roadside and stared, fixated on the empty ribbon of
highway stretched out before her. Over the rise the truck
appeared. It was unclear whether it was military. Big letters
on the side were a good sign. It was hard to make them
out until it got closer. UNHCR. No one flinched. Lorries from
humanitarian aid groups had passed by us before, always
packed to capacity with the sickest people who had been

on foot, pregnant mothers, small children. But those lorries never stopped.

This one did.

The driver pulled over to the side of the road. None of us moved a muscle, as if holding our collective breath at the possibility that the truck might be stopping for us. All these months we had had no protection from any government agency or humanitarian group. It was hard to believe that would change. But the driver got out. He spoke first with an old man in our group who was on the verge of collapse. Maybe they would just take him. In the truck, on the passenger side, another man got out. He opened the back of the truck. Staring back at us were women and children who sat on narrow benches that lined each side, their eyes blank from exhaustion. Like ours.

Then, one at a time, the men helped us into the truck. All of us. Kids sat on the floor, leaning against each other. Mom did not say a word, maybe in case she might jinx it. The driver secured the canvas backing, and that was that. Soon we were bouncing along the unpaved road, kids bumping shoulders as we rocked back-and-forth on the floor, some-times knocking heads when we hit potholes the size of volcanoes. Kakuma must have been close for the lorry to pick us up. At last, our journey would be over.

The old man who had gotten in the truck first sat close to Mom. She spoke to him in a low tone, but he answered out loud for all to hear what the driver had told him. Kakuma was not close. In fact, we were still in southern Sudan. After months of travel, I had begun to think that maybe we had walked right past Kakuma. But no. His next sentence almost made me want to get out. The man said we would remain in danger until we crossed the border into Kenya. Humanitarian trucks on the main route had frequently been attacked by armed bandits. At least on foot we had hidden in the dark of night. The truck was an easy target.

But I was so tired I didn't care what happened. Likali, Mom, John Udong and I, along with the rest in our group, fell fast asleep. Every few minutes we were jolted awake as we drove over those big potholes. South Sudan had few paved roads. The rainy season had taken its toll on this one, parts of which had been paved but could not hold up under the torrential rains that hammered the countryside in the wet season. Everyone would open their eyes for a moment, then fall back asleep. At least the rest of our journey would be easy. All we had to do was sit there, and pray no bandits held us up.

It was not an hour later when the truck stopped. I was disoriented, sleepy. Could we have reached Kakuma? No. A fast leak in one of the front tires made driving unsafe. One at a time we climbed down. The repair would take a while. The driver told us to keep walking, that they would catch up to us after they patched the hole. Just like that we were on foot again. And that is how our long, hot, dusty, bumpy trip to Kakuma progressed, the truck breaking down at regular intervals and us walking again on foot in daylight on the open road, something we had managed to avoid for five years wandering southern Sudan.

At night we slept in open space near the road, the truck with big letters next to us for protection. I was so hungry, so tired, that once my legs stopped moving, I fell asleep quickly like the other children, our bodies depleted. My biggest fear, other than being lost and never reaching the camp, was that we would reach it, but it would be full because it had taken us so long. Then we would have to get back in the truck and drive somewhere else, maybe Uganda or Ethiopia, which we would never reach because the truck would break down for good and we would be on foot again. Mom assured me we would indeed reach Kakuma, and there would be room for us.

Southern Sudan was, in fact, much bigger than I ever imagined.

It was two weeks later that we arrived at the processing center in Lokichogio. Kenya, at last. The camp was smack on the border, administered by the United Nations High Commissioner for Refugees (UNHCR) and fell under the jurisdiction of the Kenyan government. Crossing the border into Kenya meant we would now officially be in a new category of displaced people. A new title would be added to my name in addition to that of daughter, sister, friend, cousin. I would officially a refugee, "a person who has fled her home due to political persecution, war, famine, and other causes of forced migration. The moment they cross the borders of foreign lands, migrants are known as refugees."

The word itself sounded foreign. At the time it meant little to me since everyone else was referred to as the same thing. It was only a few years later when the world began coming into focus that the deeper implication took shape—as a refugee I had no country, no real home, was dependent on aid organizations for my existence, had few rights, was assumed to have no future...and lived in a place called Nowhere.

In Nyal the roar of men cheering brought me back to the present. Rescuers had succeeded in getting the lorry out of the mud and into the middle of the road. The grinning driver climbed down, thanking the townsfolk, everyone smiling and slapping backs at a job well done. My focus returned to the clinic. As I waved to Theresa and walked back, a surge of painful emotion side-swiped my gut, muted by the light-hearted banter behind me.

That part of my story—getting to Kakuma—had happened such a long time ago. Yet these memory flashes that came in no chronological order brought feelings so intense it might have happened last week. All these years I believed that the passage of time would create distance, dull the emotions I was feeling right now. Remembering an incident was one thing. I had no interest in reliving experiences I would rather forget, the worst kind of time travel.

Inside, the clinic was still quiet. Clean beds sat waiting for patients. At the end of the hallway the supply racks stood filled with wares. I took a deep breath. This was my world now. I was a healer, no longer helpless against those who took innocent lives, but a doctor saving them.

I pulled the computer chair closer to the screen and clicked ENTER to jar it from sleep mode. Then I began typing.

7

LIKALI

Nyal, South Sudan

My room in Nyal outside the clinic is shaded by a cluster of trees that keeps it cool, a refuge following long days of a hectic pace that seems to come in spurts. The last few days had been especially busy with the usual diseases we treat at the clinic—malaria, sexually transmitted infections, and bilharzia, a parasitic disease spread by contact with fresh water that has been infested with the flatworm parasite. Children here often swim in an area of the Nyal River contaminated with the worm-carrying snails. Second only to malaria in Africa, bilharzia could be avoided altogether if we had access to medication recommended by the World Health Organization that can be given to entire high-risk groups once a year. But in rural Nyal, we do not have that medication. We must treat each case individually.

My body tightened with the recurring frustration of what could have been done if only we had the kind of access to health care needed to treat these diseases. That was the biggest obstacle. There were others that posed challenges even the World Health Organization could not overcome. Getting patients to the clinic was the first hurdle. Dealing with ambivalence once they arrived often presented the next. Ingrained tribal practices were not easy to breach. Villagers had been taking care of themselves for centuries, dying from common illnesses, delivering babies in their huts, premature death accepted as a brutal reality, as much a part of life as the changing seasons.

My biggest uphill battle was gaining the trust of my patients in the community—parents whose children required routine vaccinations; mothers who needed pre-natal care for a better outcome; diabetics who could not control their blood sugar. But mothers were suspicious of needle-bearing health workers waiting to vaccinate their children who showed no sign of being sick. Pregnant women had delivered their babies at home for eons, knowing they or their babies might die.

Prevention in any setting has its own challenges, let alone a rural village where people have done without healthcare as long as anyone could remember, except for the shamans who had treated them with inconsistent outcomes. Healthy people have little motivation to prevent what they cannot see, what has not yet happened. Why change a lifestyle or take medicine for something that may or may not occur?

Nobody wanted to hear that hand washing was the single most important prevention for the spread of food-borne disease within a household. It was too simple to go to that trouble when viruses and bacteria were invisible to the naked eye. So we did not see patients for an illness that could have been prevented, or for those already sick whose suffering we could have mitigated with proper treatment at an early stage. Patients who arrived at our clinic were often in desperate straits.

Taker is a case in point, a strapping twenty-year old male brought in by his mother. He presented with confusion, fever, and had been refusing to eat. I admitted him. Lab results were positive for malaria. I administered intravenous Artesunate, the protocol medicine for malaria. But within an hour Taker was unconscious. It was times like these that the pressure of being the sole physician in the region weighed on me. In medical school there was always someone to brainstorm with, or to talk through a problem to get that second opinion, or to assure myself if nothing else. Now it was just me making a million decisions every day on my own. Then I recalled that in med school, it was not me reaching out, but my colleagues who usually came to me to confirm a diagnosis or review a medical regimen.

What was it about me that made people assume that I could handle the weight of their problems on my shoulders? Perhaps my quiet demeanor was misinterpreted as confidence. More often than not, it was anything but. Even now I had moments of self-doubt. The consequence of my missing a telltale symptom, of not being thorough enough on exam, of tripping up on any number of things was a pressure I lived with every day. But to look at me no one would ever have known. I had long ago learned to keep my feelings inside. Whatever the reason others saw strength in me, I had carried the burden of responsibility for as long as I could remember, even as a four-year-old. I chalked it up to being the oldest among my siblings, mother's little helper from an early age. Maybe that explains why I have never felt young, much less carefree. At any rate, alone in Nyal as the only doctor for miles around, I would have to get used to making hard calls on my own.

When the young man, Taker, did not respond to the malaria medication and became unconscious, I tested his blood sugar. It was dangerously low at 1.8mmol/litre, where normal is 3.9—6mmol/litre. After infusing him with dextrose, he awoke briefly but remained confused. I suspected his blood sugar was too low for his vessels to process the dextrose. I needed to insert a nasogastric tube, or NG tube, a plastic cylinder that goes in through the nose, past the throat and down the esophagus into the stomach—the only way to deliver nutrients, meds or other oral agents in an unconscious patient, or one too weak to take them on his own.

Watching the intubation of a three-foot long tube through a loved one's nose is not an easy sight for family. But Taker's mother was undaunted, driven by her concern at his serious condition. He remained in a coma on and off. She asked if she could feed him herself. I hesitated at first, but decided that if she could do it, we could use her help. I demonstrated the NG tube insertion process so she could see the pace and angle of infusion. It turned out she was a quick study and took over feeding her son through the NG tube.

I monitored his blood sugar hourly until it stabilized. Still, he remained in a state of semi-consciousness for ten days. The clinic was not set up to treat such a sick patient with no intensive care unit, which is exactly where Taker should have been under such circumstances. Even had there been an ICU within an hour or two, Taker was in no position to travel, which was a moot point since we could not transfer him. And so he remained in the clinic.

All of us were pulling for him, the entire clinic staff — James Bouk, Daniel Deng, Simon Yul, and Peter Kor in pharmacy, concocting his nutrients and meds. It was touch-and-go, Taker's semi-conscious state not improving. Then it did. He began to respond to treatment. He was able to eat. Ten days after he was brought in, Taker walked out of the clinic under his own steam. What a triumph!

Of course, it could have gone either way. We knew that. But this one hadn't. Moments like these were ones I tucked away for later, successes I would draw on when the next seriously ill patient showed up at our clinic because there was no other facility available. In Nyal there would be ample opportunity to test my mettle as a physician. Taker had been a success story—one I would recall when cursed with self-doubt. I knew they would not all end that way.

It was a few months later, in February, that we were tested again. This time it was children we admitted, four of them in two days, all between the ages of six months and two years, all suffering from severe diarrhea. It was paramount that we stop the acute watery diarrhea to avoid extreme fluid loss. Keeping the children clean and hydrated until we could accomplish that required a team effort, during which I monitored their labs. I knew a food or water-borne illness was the cause, and that these admits would not be the only ones.

By the end of the week, our patient census had ballooned from four children to twenty, all in the same age range of six months to two years, all severely dehydrated. Many of them were also in hypovolemic shock, a critically dangerous situation in which extreme fluid loss renders the heart unable to pump enough blood to the body, which can cause organ failure—which is how Likali died, the same intense, explosive diarrhea rapidly depleting her body.

Extreme dehydration also meant our young patients' peripheral veins were collapsed. Normally, inserting an IV for rapid fluid replacement would be the first measure, but it was too late for that. Collapsed veins would not take a needle, no matter how small. And a small needle would not be sufficient. Plan B involved inserting an intravenous cannular line, basically a narrow tube extending the length of a regular needle, to push fluids and medication directly into the bloodstream through the larger jugular veins on the neck or those on the scalp. These could be tricky to keep in place with squirmy kids, but our young patients were too sick to protest, too weak to cry. Their mothers gathered outside the clinic every day, the group expanding with each new admission, each mother keeping vigil to see if her child would survive.

The outbreak pushed the limits of our clinic to the edge. For three solid weeks we worked from seven in the morning until eleven at night. Then two rotating nurses would cover the night shift. It did not matter where a member of the team usually worked. We pulled together as one unit, the only feasible way to cope with the outbreak, all of us on duty Monday through Sunday. No one said it out loud, but in the back of our minds we understood the biggest threat to successful treatment, that resources—medication, supplies, IV fluids—were limited. Nyal being Nyal—no replacements would be arriving. We had someone washing linens on every shift. We kept a close watch on supplies, using up the reserves in our storage room.

After three weeks working around the clock, the first children were discharged, reunited with their weary, exhausted mothers. Over the next week, more patients followed. By the end of the fourth week, all had been sent home. Twenty children had been admitted to the clinic with severe dehydration. Twenty children had been discharged home with their mothers. My clinic staff was exhausted too, all of us. But our hearts were full, satisfied that we had done our best, grateful that our best had been enough. I felt especially gratified.

Throughout the ordeal, in every child's face I saw my beautiful little sister. I still remember the awful helplessness that gripped me that day. As a doctor I now know It was unreasonable to think that I could have saved my sister that day. The bacteria that infested her body had done its damage by the time she went into cramps. In my mind I understood that. My heart was another story.

We were living in Kakuma. I was six, Likali, three. Mom often left me in charge of my siblings when she had to get our food or water. That particular day she had gone to the river. Watching Likali was hardly a chore since we played together constantly. The girl rarely let me out of her sight. That morning she was sitting in the dirt, legs spread, using a twig to draw roads across the countryside represented by a big circle marked by the length of her tiny legs, or as far as she could reach, and from knee to knee. A smooth rock served as a truck, with her as driver.

In Likali's country, the truck tires never went flat. She boasted the roads were so smooth no one ever felt a bump. Whatever pretend stories she made up in that young mind of hers, she delighted in the fantasy, her sing-song voice chatting away in a narrative only she understood. It was lovely background chatter. Then she went silent, falling over sideways in the dirt, pulling her legs close to her body in a fetal position while gasping in pain. Within a minute she was experiencing explosive watery diarrhea. She whimpered in misery.

For two hours it was all I could do to keep Likali clean, changing her soiled clothes into whatever other clothes I could find until I had used up most of hers and mine. In desperation I tried to get her to drink water. She turned her face away. Even as a child I understood that her insides were pouring out, that it had to be stopped.

In the camp, Peter was like a magician to us kids. Whenever a neighbor suffered any number of maladies, it was Peter we turned to. The young man could cure minor ailments with potions or herbs. Leaving my sister curled on the ground, I ran to get him. But Peter was nowhere to be found. Our refugee camp had grown by thousands, shacks as far as the eye could see. There was no time to search beyond my immediate neighborhood. I ran back to Likali. By then she was barely conscious. Mom, returning from the river, walked toward us. In the distance she could see us huddled outside the hut. Mom must have known something was very wrong because she broke into a run.

Telling me to stay with Udong, she scooped my limp unconscious sister into her arms and rushed toward the clinic, which was clear on the other side of the camp. I watched until she disappeared. I hardly breathed, my eyes fixated on the path my mother took, the one she and Likali would return on. The day seemed oddly normal, sun piercing through white puffy clouds. Udong napped inside. It was quiet, or maybe I just didn't hear anything, trying to imagine what was happening with my sister, oblivious to everything around me. *Please God, please help Likali.*

Heat made the air wavy, distorting my vision. I strained to see a figure coming up the road in the distance. It was Mom. Alone. Had they kept Likali at the clinic? I ran to Mom, but already knew the answer. Mom's shoulders were hunched, tears streaming down her face, a moan of anguish filling the air like a wounded animal. She was unsteady on her feet, as if she might collapse any moment under the crushing weight of such sorrow. My mind swirled trying to process the obvious— that my little sister would not be coming home. My lungs closed. I struggled to breathe.

I managed to grab onto Mom as we stumbled inside the house, holding each other. I did not think one heart could bear as much pain as mine did that day. Then anguish turned to anger. How could God be so cruel? I had so many questions, questions I could not ask because there was no answer. Why did she have to get sick? Why had God taken my sister after all we had been through, all we had survived getting to Kakuma? Why now? Why Likali? Why could the clinic not save her? Why had I not acted sooner? How could I go on? I was inconsolable.

But I did go on, my grief buried deep inside. I slept. I ate. I waited at the bor hole for water—all the usual things I had done every day, as if no one noticed that I had fallen into a giant crack in the earth. I saw Likali's body before she was taken for burial. It was the most helpless feeling I ever experienced. She had trusted me to take care of her. Mom had trusted me.

In my heart I promised both of them that one day I would become a doctor. Never again would a child in my care die from something that could have been prevented in the first place, if not easily treated with medicine. I would live in a place that had clean water, a place where water nurtures life rather than takes it. To this day when I stand at a bor tap, watching water flow into my pail, I see life flowing out. The same way it flowed out of my sister.

My promise was made in anger in those raw moments of utter despair. But it stayed with me through eighteen years of education—from St. Bakhita's to Mount Kenya University Medical School. Somehow I believed that If I could save one child's life, it might make up for not saving Likali's. I know that was not rational. Nothing would ever make up for her death. But I needed to prove to myself that all my years of unforgiving obstacles and the desperate struggle to stay in school had been worth the financial investment others had made in me. Worth the years of silent anguish that I had suffered in her loss.

Until that day in Nyal after the outbreak when the last child left the clinic, I had never considered that preventing a death is not the same thing as saving a life. The outcome is the same, of course. But the experience is not. One has to do with the trauma of losing my sister, a vindication, a tallying of the score. A re-do, however irrational that sounds. I had never considered the flip side—the sheer joy of saving a life, the heady power in averting tragedy for an entire community, knowing that no mother would have to experience what mine had. That no sister would devote her life making up for what she never could have done as a six-year-old child. Like I had.

I owed Likali a great debt. I believe that day at the clinic it was paid in full. I had saved a child's life. Twenty times over.

Photos courtesy of Kenneth Waxman, M.D.

8

LIFE IN KAKUMA

Northwest Kenya

Dust storms are a regular occurrence in the barren camp, especially in the afternoon. In addition to food and clothes, UNHCR had given us palm leaves to function as a roof, and construction poles for the mud house we would construct. Some people had crafted roofs from oil tins, a luxury in a land where rainstorms can sweep houses away, to say nothing of drenching everything under a palm-leaf roof. Mom and I constructed our shelter in little time. Future "remodels" would follow. But I hated the dust and had had enough of it for a lifetime.

There were no bathrooms in Kakuma. That came as no surprise in a camp hastily constructed and quickly overcome with hordes of refugees with no time to build anything, or money or materials to do it with. To this day there is no sewage system. Refugees dig a hole a few meters from their house, which UNHCR workers cover with cement, leaving an opening on top. The holes are deep, and once they reach capacity, workers close it down and refugees dig another hole.

Twenty years later, there are still no bathrooms, but the modern version of holes behind the house consists of sheltered areas built using aluminum sheets for protection and privacy. This also serves as a shower facility where people carry their own water in a bucket for bathing.

Water was as precious then as it is now. We got ours from the taps that opened twice a day for two hours, each tap serving a specific neighborhood and no

one else. At six in the morning the tap would open. Mom or me and Likali would get in line as early as four and wait. The tap opened again at four in the afternoon for two hours. As long as we had water to drink us kids did not care that we lived with a fine coat of dust covering our clothes and skin, the barren windswept camp making it impossible to stay clean for long. Mom kept a bucket of water to wash us before bed every night. That was the best she could do.

Every fifteen days the UNHCR handed out rations of wheat flour, maize flour, porridge flour, salt, beans, peas and oil. Sugar was a rarity. My mom used to sell oil so she could buy sugar and meat, which we ate once a month. Mom is the most inventive person I have ever known. She could turn any mix of ingredients into a tasty meal. We knew it. Others in the camp knew it too.

Market in Gogrial. Photo courtesy of Kenneth Waxman, M.D.

When one aid group caught wind of Mom's skills, they hired her as a cook. That meant she was able to buy or trade for food we had been missing in our diets. As agriculture was almost impossible in the desolate terrain—the driest, hottest, most infertile corner of Kenya—competition was fierce among different local groups for ownership of cattle. Refugees were not allowed to keep animals, due to the potential for conflict between us and the local Turkana people, who resented what they thought was better treatment of refugees—food and healthcare from the UNHCR, which was more than they got from their own government.

There were two churches in our area, one African, right behind our house where it still stands today. Mom belonged to that congregation. The other house of worship was Catholic. Some refugees, especially children, attended services every Sunday. Practicing our religion in this structured manner was the first real stability in our day-to-day lives that I could remember in my short life. For so long we had made our own community of fellow refugees with no structure or institutions. Having them in place added to a sense of being in the civilized world where people prospered and took care of their families and thought about the future. To say that about a refugee camp tells you something about how we had lived for five of my six years, in constant uncertainty that we would have basic food and shelter, much less any thought of a stable future.

As Mom promised, Kakuma was a better place than where we had been. But after Likali died, a heavy, oppressive sadness hung over me. Whatever hardships we had experienced in Torit, or anywhere else, paled in comparison to life without my sister. The world had turned dark. I saw everything through a veil, the landscape colorless, a blurry endless grey. John Udong could not understand why Likali was no longer there to play with him. She had brought joy to everyone, especially to me and Udong. Her absence was unbearable. But God was about to give us a gift, a gift that would help us begin to heal.

When we had first arrived at the refugee camp, my father had visited for a few days before disappearing again. Had I been older it might have dawned on me. I

was too little to make a connection between his visit and my mother's pregnancy. Four long, awful months after we lost Likali, out of the wasteland that was Kakuma, Karoline Achii was born. My father returned a few days before her birth, which made her entry into this world a very happy occasion.

Three days after his visit he returned to southern Sudan. There was no way I could have known it at the time, but that visit would be the last time I saw my father. I still held on to the belief that when the fighting stopped, he would come for us. That would never happen. In the meantime, I focused on the baby, a beautiful girl with a smile so like that of Likali's that I knew my little sister was with us somehow, would always be with us, reflected in Karoline Achii's smile.

In Kakuma there was also a school. The teacher held classes outside while a real adobe schoolhouse was being built to accommodate the ever- increasing influx of refugees. But in 1995, it would still be a while before my formal education began. I did not go to school. Mom needed me to stay home and help with the baby and Udong. That was okay with me. A lot of boys went to school but not many girls. Most stayed at home to help. Education was not valued in a culture where most girls grew up to get married and have children. That was not going to be me. My promise to Likali was not going to fizzle out in a few months. Forged in the depths of despair, that vow became a part of me. I carried my sister in my heart and knew one day I would get my chance to go to school.

In 1997 I got that chance. Starting primary 1 at the age of eight I was older than most of the kids in that grade. That did not bother me. Kakuma was filled with childhoods thrown off track by war. No one cared how old you were in which grade. We had survived. Everything else was a bonus. Like school. Especially school.

Agwak, education is the way to a better life. Mom had repeated that countless times. I was not sure why or how education gave you a better life. In my six-year-old mind, a better life meant the one we had before we fled Torit, when I was oblivious to everything, happy playing with Likali and my friends, cooking with

my mother, carrying Udong around in my arms, his feet dragging as he giggled. By the time I was eight, I knew Mom meant that there was a world beyond Torit, beyond Kakuma, where people did not have to scrape by for survival, where food was consistently available. A world where children did not die of treatable diseases. I wanted to find that path to a better life.

And so I began that long, long journey, starting with primary 1. For six hours a day I was transported to that other world. There is not much to do in a refugee camp, no place you can go beyond the fence. I had been lucky having Udong and Achii to take care of. In school I was also distracted from hunger. Humanitarian groups did their best but there was never enough food with the ever-increasing number of refugees. Hunger was worse at night while trying to fall asleep. School and church

were the two places where I could overcome my growling stomach, where I was able to sense that bigger world Mom talked about. One thing confused me though.

Education may have been the way to a better life, but how did I get there from a classroom in a refugee camp? The answer would come in the most unexpected way.

By the time I was twelve, I had reached primary 5. In the classroom, Angela, my best friend, sat behind me. When she got bored with our lessons, which was often, she would whisper into the back of my head all the romantic things boys would say to me. I did not dare giggle in class. The twelve-year-old boys of Angela's imagination courted me with compliments on my beauty, my athleticism in racing them around camp. Sometimes they praised my intelligence, but Angela liked to leave that one out of her fantasy scenarios. She was not a good student, and in her daydreams, boys came before education.

It had not occurred to me as a child that without a future to plan for, dreams were small, futures already determined by cultural norms, and in our case, the limits of a refugee camp. Likali's death had forged my destiny. It turned out that feeling helpless, for me, was intolerable. I had no idea how I would become a doctor. It was unfathomable. But never for one day did I believe it could not be done. My ignorance turned out to be a blessing—better not to see the mountain I had to climb, better just to take the first step, and never look back.

Angela's dreams did not reach beyond the perimeter of our desolate world. They were constructed on life as we knew it, a more realistic dream than my outlandish fantasy. My friend dreamed of building a big store in Kakuma filled with all kinds of things—dresses and glitter and sunglasses, school supplies—enough pencils that we didn't have to break them in half. Every few months the store would become more elaborate as she added a soda machine, jewelry. The particulars of how Angela would create this imaginary store were never clear. Money would fall from the sky as far as I could tell. It didn't matter. To dream of a better existence at all kept us going. Angela's store was the stuff of hope.

Other than school, I most looked forward to going to church every Sunday. A man named Patrick Ubaa, a catechist in the Catholic church, had created a girls' choir. I loved to sing. Mine was a clear sweet voice. Mr. Ubaa said it was rich, emotive. Not only that, he said I was a mezzo-soprano, a singer who could reach the highest notes. In almost every song, when the range went above a certain octave, my voice was the only one heard. When the choir sang in unison as one voice, I levitated, lifted right out of this world into one where Likali was with us again, my dad too—all of us a family, whole, living in a peaceful place where the soil was rich, trees lush, water abundant, lots of cows. And no dust.

One Sunday I got to do a solo in front of the whole congregation, a song of praise, thanks, like a prayer. Silence fell over the room as everyone focused on me. A feeling of joy bubbled up inside, as if God Himself were looking down on all of us with His grace filling the church. After the service people complimented me on my beautiful performance. I burst with pride!

As I left the church a priest approached me. He had been sitting in the back. I did not recognize him as one of the priests I had seen before. He was older with a huge shock of white hair, which made him look like a wise elder. The man stopped in front of me, hands behind his back, a big smile on his face as he leaned down.

"Hello, young lady. That was quite a performance."

"Thank you," I said smiling back, still floating in the wake of high praise from the congregants.

"Your voice is a gift."

"Thank you," I repeated, looking down at my feet, my natural shyness taking over, embarrassed by the second compliment. Sensing my discomfort, he broke into a big grin.

"I guess I should introduce myself. My name is Father Elia. I am visiting from Nairobi." He offered his right hand for me to shake. No adult had ever shaken my hand. I looked at his, then reached out. "And may I ask your name?"

"Hellen. Hellen Onyango."

"Well, Miss Onyango, besides singing in church, do you go to school?"

"Yes." Then he went on to ask about my classes, how did I like them, was I a good student, had I ever thought about what I might like to do someday? I had no idea why he asked these questions, beyond polite curiosity. But all I had done was sing. That hardly made me the choir ambassador. Yet he spoke to me like an adult, as if we were conversing about world issues, with not an ounce of condescension. My initial shyness dissipated. I decided that I liked this Father Elia from Nairobi.

"In addition to your voice, Hellen, I was struck by your composure. You seem like a girl who is quite mature for her age. Would you say that describes you?"

I answered with a half-shrug.

"I expect it does." Then he glanced around the church. "Is your mother here with you?"

"No, she...she goes to a different service."

"Ah. Would it be alright with you if I met her?"

My stomach tightened. Mom had gone to a different service alright. She was a member of the African Church behind our house, and attended every Sunday, including this one. If Father Elia had hopes of converting her to Catholicism, he was wasting his time. Mom descended from many generations that worshiped our Pari gods, people who had no use for the Catholicism brought to Africa by eighteenth-century missionaries who had forced it on everyone.

But in Kakuma there were a lot of people who attended the African church. Why would the priest single Mom out if he were trying to convert someone? That could not be it. At any rate, he was a nice man. I led him to my house, terribly curious about what in the world a Catholic priest from Nairobi would have to say to my mom.

She glanced at me with one eyebrow slightly raised when I introduced him at the door as the Catholic priest from church. With a polite smile, she stepped aside for him to enter. Over tea he again said what a beautiful voice I had. Mom had never made much fuss over any of us kids, though I knew she agreed with him about my voice.

"Mrs. Onyango," he said, setting his teacup on the low table. "Hellen tells me she does well in school, though I sense modesty."

I opened my eyes wide at Mom, tilting my head in mock curiosity to see what she would say.

"Hellen has always done well with her studies. She gets high marks from her teachers." Mom glanced at me with my expectant look awaiting more details from her about my intelligence, my maturity. "In fact, Hellen has always been more interested in studying than spending time with girls her age."

What? That was it, the totality of her singing my praises? Father Elia probably thought I was the most unpopular girl in all of Kakuma...'Hellen has always been more interested in studying than spending time with girls her age?' I cringed, then looked at Father Elia.

The priest stared into his teacup, as if seeing the future in soaked tea leaves at the bottom. Elbows on his knees, he leaned forward and addressed both of us.

"I'm involved with a Catholic boarding school in Narus, about an hour north of here...St. Bakhita's Day and Boarding Girls' Primary School. It has only been in existence six years, run by the Sisters of Mary Mother of the Church of the Torit Catholic diocese."

Mom and I looked at each other, faces blank, wondering what this could possibly have to do with me.

"You are both wondering what this has to do with Hellen," he chuckled. "Well, the school was established with the mission of helping girls of southern Sudan whose schooling has been disrupted by the war."

That would be just about every girl in the country. Why me?

As if he had read my mind, he went on. "I'm offering sponsorship to a few girls who meet the criteria as

117

candidates—girls who would do well academically, and just as important, girls who would stay the course and finish their primary education."

The ones more interested in studying than being with girls their own age, he means. It took me a moment to grasp what it was exactly the priest was offering.

Mom lifted her chin with an unapologetic look. "Father, I appreciate your interest in my daughter, but we have no money to pay for a boarding school."

He means me? Sending me to boarding school? With proper books and teachers and classes for each grade level? A thrill shot through me.

"I apologize for not explaining....there would be no cost. I'm offering this sponsorship to five girls with my own funds...savings from my salary."

Priests get a salary?

"I believe Hellen would be an excellent candidate. She enjoys school, works hard, does well...and I suspect has the level of maturity the girls will need." He paused, looking at each of us.

"One of the biggest challenges girls face is being separated from their families eleven months out of the year...

January to December...with a four-week holiday break for Christmas."

He let that sink in.

"As you know, transportation between Narus and Kakuma is difficult because of the road conditions during the rainy season...and dangerous. Random bandits

regularly attack even the NGO supply trucks. The safest course is to have the girls stay at the school all year except for Christmas holiday."

Mom jerked her head back with a look of surprise. Father Elia shifted in his chair. "I realize Hellen is only twelve. Being away from home for such long stretches may be more than either of you wants to consider." He looked at Mom.

"I see."

No! We want to consider it! I sat up straight, facing Mom. She stared past me, lost in thought. Mentally I sped through the pros and cons that I knew she was weighing. I would be able to finish my primary education in a proper school...a religious environment, nuns likely to be strict like her. It would cost her nothing...plus, there would be one less mouth to feed. On the other hand, she would not have me to take care of Udong and Achii after school while she was at work.

119

But Mom would add another reason to the pro column, maybe the most important one—girls my age in Kakuma often got pregnant, which meant the end of school. Once pregnant, the girl went to live with the boy's family, ending all hope of further education. If a married man fathered the baby, the girl went to live in his household as a domestic while raising the child. Either way, no more school.

Mom trusted me to steer clear of boys. But next year I would be a teenager. I know she worried about that. But foremost in her mind as she made her decision would be the rare opportunity Father Elia was offering. *Agwak, education is the key to a better life.* Mom's silence lasted only a few moments. She turned to me with a slight smile, eyes narrow slits in a private communication to convey her answer before addressing the priest. I understood that look immediately and smiled back.

And so that very Sunday evening, I packed my few belongings and said goodbye to Udong and Achii, who would be fast asleep when I left early the next morning. In our culture we have a tradition in which elders sprinkle water on travelers to protect them from harm. Mom had invited a few of them to bless me and the four other girls who had been selected. At dawn the next morning the little group gathered in front of our house for the blessing. Fifteen minutes later, in the early light of day, the five of us heading to St. Bakhita's huddled together at the bus stop, about to face the unknown at a school we had never heard of in a city far away from home. What we did know is that we had been offered the greatest opportunity of our young lives.

We were leaving the Land of Nowhere for the Land of Possibilities.

How could I have known that when Father Elia visited Kakuma that Sunday afternoon his conversation with Mom would change my life forever. The moment I stepped on that bus to Narus, I had taken the first step toward my future—a journey of eighteen years. But I would get there.

One tiny step at a time.

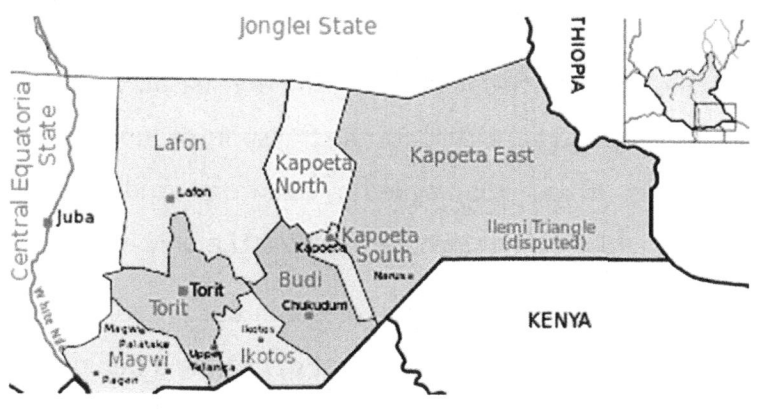

Narus, Kapoeta South

9

ST. BAKHITA'S

Narus, South Sudan

We sat close together waiting for the bus, each with our box of worldly belongings, sleepy from the early departure. There was only one highway on the Kenyan northern corridor—the road from Kapoeta to Lokichogio, the town where the refugee processing center was located, the very one where Mom and Likali and Udong and I had stayed for three weeks when we arrived in Kakuma six years earlier. In the rainy season the Narus River flooded, cutting off the town. Luckily, we were traveling during the dry season when the gravel road was accessible for the transport of supplies and personnel. It was still plagued by risk from bandits, cattle rustlers and rebel fighters. But that was the only road.

At sixteen, Akera was the oldest in our group, making her our leader by default. The rest of us trailed behind her outside the processing center as she inquired about a vehicle going to Narus, one that could give us a ride. There was none. We had no idea where we would sleep that night if we could not get to the school. We sat on the ground outside and waited. And waited. And waited.

Around three in the afternoon, a lorry pulled into the Lokichogio processing centre. Akera watched the driver get out, then approached him. She explained that we were students trying to get to St. Bakhita's in Narus. Luck was with us. He was on his way to Narus to deliver food. There was room in his truck. It was only sixteen miles, a one-hour drive from Northern Kenya, but by the time we arrived, twelve hours would pass since leaving Kakuma that morning.

The drive felt longer than it might have had we not been so worn out and hungry. A lifetime had passed since church services on Sunday morning the previous day. The truck bounced too much on the bumpy road to get any sleep. The same potholes I remembered on the final leg of our journey to Kakuma made for slow going, that and watching the speed so the truck would not overheat and break down.

Narus town square in the 1990s

Finally, in the distance we saw signs of civilization. The driver took us all the way into town, where we thanked him, eager to get out of the truck. I felt as if someone were holding a pillow over my face. Sudan is hot. You get used to it.

In Narus it was stifling, the air oppressive. But in Narus, January and February are the hottest months, as I would soon discover. Only an hour away, if we had good transportation and safe roads, but a whole other climate compared with Kakuma. Our momentary shock gave way to giggles of relief at having reached our destination. In no time we would be walking through the door of St. Bakhita's.

It dawned on all of us that we had no idea where St. Bakhita's was. I had imagined Narus as a small town, imagined that the mighty St. Bakhita's would be the central building, bigger than the rest. But Narus was not small, despite its being deserted in the heat of late evening when we arrived. It was not quite dark, but the school was nowhere in sight. We looked at each other, uncertainty on our faces. Sticky with sweat in just the few minutes it had taken for our predicament to set in, we began asking locals for directions. Some eyed us with suspicion. Others turned away, paying no attention to the five out-of-town girls standing in the street asking for directions to a Catholic boarding school.

At last a young woman approached us. She was not much older than Akera, who explained our situation. The young woman smiled reassuringly, then motioned us to follow. She pointed out the school and then we parted. When we reached it, the place was deserted. Akera tried the gate. Locked. Walking in one direction, then the other, we spotted the gate man, who reluctantly let us through after hearing our plight. The gate had not yet closed behind us when the front door flew open. A fierce looking nun bolted out, gliding toward us as if on skates. Her face was contorted into a frown, eyes dark with anger. I was not easily frightened, but instinctively took a step backward. It was clear this nun was not St. Bakhita's Welcome Committee.

"Who are you and what are you doing here?"

Akera cleared her throat and straightened her shoulders. Stepping forward, in a calm even tone she looked the nun right in the eyes.

"Perhaps if we could speak to the Headmistress—"

"I am the Headmistress…Sister Victoria. What do you want? Why are you here at this hour?" She quickly looked us up and down. "This is not a refugee center. We have no food to give you."

Akera maintained a respectful tone. "Sister, we are from Kakuma Refugee Camp. Father Elia sent us here." The four of us nodded to confirm her story. "Our late arrival," Akera continued without missing a beat, "is due to the difficulty we had finding transport from Lokichogio. It has been a very long day of travel."

The nun's stiffened arms folded across her chest. She spoke in a tone of indignation, "Well, I have had no news of your arrival. School is not yet in session...we are not prepared for students. You can't show up at this hour, unannounced, and expect to stay."

Akera fell back a step, as if she had been punched. We stared at the nun. Her mouth in a grimace, she made it clear the conversation was over. Boxes in hand, we retraced our steps back to town, as lost as when we had stepped off the truck. Akera tried to cheer us up. "We'll be fine. We got this far, didn't we? Tomorrow we can figure things out at the school." No one spoke, too tired and discouraged to agree or disagree. I knew that Akera didn't know any better than any of us what would happen tomorrow, but her words assured me, the same way those of my mother had so long ago. *Just get to that next tree, Agwak, then we will rest.*

By this time it was dark, and we had no idea where we would sleep for the night. But Akera was right. We had gotten this far, fending for ourselves so long that together we knew it would be fine. Alone in the street, we looked around, hoping some solution would appear by magic.

She did. Seeing we were not locals, a woman passing by approached us. She spoke in a caring voice. "My name is Paulina. I live here. Why are you walking at night with your boxes? Are you lost?"

For the third time since leaving home that morning, we explained our situation, each of us taking turns recounting the story of how we were from Kakuma headed for St. Bakhita's Boarding School, how we had been stranded most of the day in Lokichogio until we got a ride with a truck driver, how a stranger had shown us to the school, ending the sad tale with the Headmistress chasing us away, which was how we ended up in the street, lost in the dark. Paulina's mouth opened slightly in disgust by the end at how we had been treated. Then she put one hand on Akera's shoulder, one on mine, and turned us around in the other direction.

"We'll go to my house. You can all spend the night. Tomorrow I'll take you to the school myself." At her house, Paulina showed us where to wash up, then disappeared into the kitchen. After eating a small meal, she led us to the room where we would sleep. Stomach full, body exhausted, I thanked God that like the truck driver before her, this woman had been there to help us. Then I fell fast asleep.

The next morning we woke around seven to the smell of porridge. Refreshed by sleep, food, and cleaned up, we trotted behind Paulina to St Bakhita's. This time the gate was open. Akera knocked on the door. Sister Victoria opened it, the angry power of authority in her eyes until she caught sight of the local woman standing behind us. When she spoke, her tone was a complete turnaround from the previous night.

"Good morning. You girls look familiar. Might you be the ones who stopped by late last night?"

Stopped by? As if it had been a social call for tea?

We nodded collectively.

"What a misunderstanding we had," she said in a saccharine voice, no doubt having considered what would happen if we told Father Elia about her chasing us away. "I had been expecting five girls from Kakuma but was certain Father Elia himself would bring them here."

As it turned out, the priest was in Kampala. There had never been any plan for him to bring us to Narus. In her mistaken assumption, Sister Victoria had been perfectly willing to turn away five girls into the night to fend for themselves in a strange town. Completely devoid of humility in her error, she puffed her chest out.

"Well, you managed to get yourselves here. What clever girls you are." She looked at Paulina, a curt nod indicating she would take it from here. We turned to Paulina with warm thanks for her hospitality. As Akera closed the gate behind Paulina, she swiveled around to Sister Victoria with a righteous glare, punctuating the contrast between our Good Samaritan whose Christian behavior had saved us from a night on the street, and the nun's own uncharitable act in refusing us. Sister Victoria cleared her throat, a cue that she was wiping the slate clean of our inauspicious beginning, sending the clear message that we would not be speaking of what she referred to as the misunderstanding to Father Elia.

Sister Victoria's proper welcome this time included a short introduction to the school before we were led across a wide-open space to our dormitory. A pair of two-story buildings housed students, one of which included the dining hall. Named after saints, our dorm was called St. Teresa, a long rectangular room with thirty bunk beds, fifteen on each side. Since none of the other students had arrived, we were told to choose the bed of our choice. The ones at the end of the room offered more privacy. I waited to see if anyone else headed that way.

When no one did, I quickly set my box on the last bed, upper bunk, to stake a claim.

Next the nun led us to the kitchen. She explained that we would be cooking for ourselves until the other students arrived, pointing out the available beans, lentils and maize flour. By this time in our journey, the five of us girls were comfortable together. After the nun left us, we set about preparing a meal. The kitchen fell quiet, each of us with a task. I thought about what Sister Victoria had told us during the introduction about the school's namesake—St. Bakhita. Josephine Bakhita was born in the Darfur region of Sudan in 1869. Her father had been a tribal chief. She grew up happy and prosperous during her early years in the village of her ancestors.

While still a child, only eight years old, Josephine was captured by Arab slave traders, forced to walk barefoot for 600 miles to the slave market, and sold to a Turkish general. Her treatment was harsh, the general's wife inflicting great suffering, including having her maid torture the girl by scarring her with a blade and rubbing salt in the wound to make it permanent. The name "Bakhita," which means "fortunate," was given to her in sarcasm by her owners.

After many years she was given to the Italian Vice Consul, who was visiting Sudan. He had been a kind master. When it came time to return to his country—across Sudan, the Red Sea, and the Mediterranean to Italy—he took Josephine with him. But shortly after arrival she was given to another family. They sent her to live with the Canossian Sisters in Venice. It was there that the twenty-one-year-old Josephine learned about God and Christianity. At the age of forty-one, she was welcomed as one of the Canossian Sisters. For the next quarter century, Sister Josephine carried out humble services in the convent—cooking, sewing, and cleaning the chapel. During World War I, she helped care for the wounded, and became known for her kindness, a source of comfort and encouragement to everyone who came to her in need.

Josephine Bakhita had been canonized in the year 2000 by Pope John Paul II, only a year before I arrived at St. Bakhita's, and became the patron saint of Christian Sudanese people who still suffered persecution for their faith. That night fixing our meal at the school, I thought about St. Bakhita, how she had walked hundreds of miles in her bare feet, not knowing if she would live or die. Like me. Unlike me, she had been beaten, tortured. But Josephine never became bitter. If this woman, who lived in slavery from childhood, whose life had been filled with so much suffering could come through years of abuse and still be strong and merciful and contribute to humanity, then I would aspire to be like her. I would pray to St. Bakhita to help me cope with being on my own and help me do well in school so that I could become a doctor and alleviate whatever suffering I could. I would dedicate my life to restoring human dignity in every patient, every person who crossed my path whose life had been decimated by war.

It would not take long for me to realize what a lofty goal I had set.

10

DESPAIR

Narus, Southern Sudan

Three days later, the other students arrived. The five of us from Kakuma had come from farthest away. The new arrivals lived in nearby villages and were collected by lorries sent from St. Bakhita's to bring them. The place felt more like a school after they came. Many of them had been going to St. Bakhita's since it first opened six years earlier. I felt out of place, not only because my home was so far away, and a refugee camp at that, but because up until this moment most of my education had taken place outside, under a tree, or in a makeshift classroom with few books or supplies. Even once we had a proper school building, there were only two teachers who covered every subject area for all of us lumped together in one classroom. But I had always done well and was used to figuring things out on my own. 'Self-motivated' was the term my teachers used. In truth, I liked having my work done quickly, then helping the little ones with their studies. My assignments never suffered because of it.

By nature I was quiet. My mother said I was more reserved than shy. When adults addressed me, I was comfortable answering. But no one would accuse me of being a social butterfly either, girls like Angela, or like some of the girls I met at my new school, always giggling and whispering and fussing with their hair. I imagined every school had kids who were snobs. St. Bakhita's was no different. It was not blatant, just an undercurrent rather than outright one-up-mans-ship. After all, St. Bakhita's was created for students impacted by the civil war, so no girl had much more than any other when it came to worldly goods.

Still, I was self-conscious. The few dresses I had were hand-me-downs from neighbors and hung loose on me. Small boned and slender, clothes seemed to drop straight from my shoulders to my knees without slowing down over protruding breasts or hips. Mom used to tie a cloth belt around my waist to give shape to the loose-fitting clothes. It didn't help that the baggy look made me seem younger.

The combination of my quiet manner and feeling self-conscious did nothing to boost my confidence. I knew that at home some girls thought I was unfriendly, or worse, a snob. Friendships during my transient life had never been long-lasting. Achii and I were so close that I had not felt the need for a lot of friends. Besides, I had Angela. She was like having three friends. At St. Bakhita's, I would have to make an effort to blend in so no one would think me standoffish. The truth was I wanted to lose myself in my studies, the only place I felt in control of my life. And that was a good place to be.

Once the entire student body was on campus, the cook prepared daily meals for everyone. When we started classes, not only did we have separate classrooms for each grade, but each subject had its own teacher too—trained educators with an established curriculum designed for a path to high school, and even beyond to college. All my teachers were so kind, keenly aware that we were the select few lucky enough to be offered a better future than 99% of girls in Sudan. They were as dedicated to giving us the best education they could as we were, committed to making the most of that opportunity. I never lost sight of the fact that it was up to me to prove myself worthy of the investment Father Elia had made in me.

As excited as I was about being at St. Bakhita's, the first few months were difficult. The countless hardships I had experienced earlier in life had been different, based on survival—staying safe travelling on foot at the mercy of armed bandits and dangerous soldiers, exposure to the elements, wildlife, Malaria. Finding enough food to eat every day, clean water to drink. Everyone had been on a level playing field. School presented a different kind of hardship. After that horrible night fleeing Torit when I got separated from Mom, I had never been away from her. Whatever suffering we had experienced, we experienced it together, along with Likali and Udon, later with Achii. Now I was on my own. The obstacles I faced at St. Bakhita's felt altogether different, and I was at a loss how to overcome them.

Overnight I was living with strangers, girls from other towns, new teachers, new rules—a different way of life that required a level of social skill that did not come naturally to me. Extroverts have an easier time of it. They put themselves out there for the world to see, tell everyone their opinions, their concerns. They laugh out loud. Introverts like me draw attention by our reserved presence, declining to share every detail of our lives with anyone who asks.

Talk. Share. Laugh. I felt pressured to be like everyone else. Whether you are left-handed or right, people accept that you were born that way. Being quiet by nature suited me, not that I liked keeping everything to myself. I did not want to act the same as other girls my age. I was not the same. I had a mission. Nothing would derail me from keeping my promise to Likali. Neither Mom nor Father Elia would know that the adjustment to boarding school was turning out to be a lot harder than anticipated. They had treated me like the mature person they expect me to be, no doubt assuming that leaving the cocoon of my family and stepping into another world would be just one more hurdle to clear like so many I had cleared in the past. But Mom had been beside me for all those hurdles. Here I was alone. This was not college. Not even high school. I was twelve years old, in primary school. And I missed my mom.

The other girls from Kakuma—Akera, Betty, and the two sisters, were in different grades. At night I watched my travel companions in our dorm, absorbed with their new friends. There were two other sisters with us in the dorm, ages five and eight, from the Murle tribe in Pibor County and Boma area in Jonglei State in South Sudan. They had already been at St. Bakhita's for two years, orphans brought to the school by Bishop Taban Paride, who first opened St. Bakhita's. The Sisters of Mary took the girls in. During holidays when other students went home, the girls stayed at the convent with the nuns. This was their home. I was in awe of that, two young girls without a family of their own. I could not imagine it.

St. Bakhita's would never feel like home, or the nuns my family. Outside of class I wanted nothing more than to be left alone to study. That didn't mean I was unfriendly. It did mean I was more comfortable in my own company than I was in making new friends. Though the distance between Kakuma and Narus was only sixteen miles as the crow flies, I might as well have been on another planet.

The academic part of school was fine, as it always had been. But how to manage the rest of my life became a bigger concern every day. Most girls do not face adult responsibilities until they get married or are old enough to work and live on their own. I was no stranger to responsibilities. At home I used to wash my own clothes as well as Achii's and Udong's. At school I had only myself to take care of, which made things easier. I had never shied away from responsibility. But money. Managing money was a brand-new experience, and I had no clue. Looking back, that first year at St. Bakhita's was the only time in my life before or since that having money presented a challenge.

The night before I left home, Mom handed me five USD to use as pocket money, a fortune, the largest amount I had ever held in my hand. It was so unexpected, I was stunned. She gave me no advice on how to budget it. Mom always bought whatever we needed from the market. Otherwise we traded goods, made them, or did without. Here I was with this windfall—five U.S. dollars—to parcel out over eleven months of school.

I decided caution would be my strategy. Acutely aware of how hard it must have been for Mom to take this amount from her earnings, I also wondered what she and Achii and

Udong would be doing without so that I could have this amount of cash. Mom would be short. She also had one less mouth to feed but would be saving money all year to pay for my transport home for the Christmas holiday break next December.

After two weeks at school, I made my first purchase—a bar of soap, but not before weighing the pros and cons. On the pro side, it was a practical investment. Soap could be used for bathing as well as washing clothes. On the con side, water was usually enough for bathing. For washing clothes, friction, rubbing fabric together, usually worked well enough. The hard part of my decision was not knowing what other needs might come up before the end of the term. Eleven months was a long time. If something came up that I needed, there would be no one to ask. I decided the soap was a multitask item.

Oh, the heady power of spending my own money! A bar of soap might have been practical, but it was also an indulgence, one that would have to last a long time. My intoxicating experience with capitalism was short lived. By the second month at school, soap was the least of my concerns. Food supplies had run short. That came as a surprise to me since the Catholic Church must have had reserves to get the school whatever it needed. Feeding 500 girls would surely have been a priority.

What began as an inconvenience continued to get worse until finally we were labouring under a severe food shortage. No one could tell us why. Then it got to the point where the school could no longer avoid an explanation—the central government had bombed the town of Narus, wiping out the food supply. Whatever wasn't demolished by the blast had been looted. The nuns had been feeding us from the reserves in storage, but the main road was impassable for trucks to deliver food. There was nothing the nuns could do. The entire community faced the same problem.

The nuns struggled to feed us anything at all—a small bowl of porridge for breakfast, a bit more for lunch. Dinner was non-existent, or rare. Whatever food was stored on campus had to last until trucks could get through, which meant the road had to be repaired. With a large student body to feed, it took little time before our cupboards were empty. The small boxes of food we had brought from home were long gone. We would have packed more had we thought there was need, but no one mentioned such a possibility.

Nor did anyone talk about other ways to get food, at least not that my classmates and I were aware of. Not that we were strangers to hunger. At home there had been plen-ty of times when food supplies ran short, rebels or bandits intercepting deliveries to the NGOs that ran Kakuma. It wasn't uncommon to miss a meal. Two, sometimes. But we had never missed all three meals in one day. Now a bowl of thin broth each day was all we had to sustain us.

It became hard to concentrate on my studies. Like everyone else, by afternoons I felt weak, by nighttime, light-headed. It was all I could do to keep any focus at all on my schoolwork with my gnawing belly demanding attention. Before my family arrived at Kakuma, we had gone months scavenging for food on our own, sometimes days passing where we had only water. But then we would get to a forest, or grasslands, or a river, some kind of access to berries or edible plants. At school we had nowhere else to look.

Late one night my Kakuma cohorts and I decided to take matters into our own hands. After everyone else in the dorm was asleep, we snuck outside and headed to the chicken coop. Chickens needed their grain maize to lay eggs. No food, no eggs. But we would not be alive to eat the eggs if we died of starvation. That was the logic that drove our decision. It was them or us, we were that desperate. On tippy toes in silence we opened the coop, careful not to rouse the chickens, and gathered up the maize in our hands. When our pockets were full, we made a stealthy beeline to the kitchen to prepare our feast. In our grand plan, there was one factor we had not considered. Field corn used for livestock was not the same as sweet corn that we eat. Field corn had a higher starch content, making the kernels much tougher. That meant that not only did the kernels have to soak in water, they had to be boiled to soften.

Taking this into account, we got started, soaking the grains. Two hours was an eternity in our desperate state. Our patience ran out. We decided that after soaking them for two hours, the boiling part of the process seemed an unnecessary luxury just for added taste. Tough or soft, the maize would save us. Soothing our screaming bellies, the grain was a king's feast. The stomachache that followed was definitely uncomfortable, but it was better than the pain of hunger. Our shortcut had been worth every minute of misery we paid in eating the tough kernels.

It didn't take long for the nuns to figure out that someone had stolen the chicken feed. By then even they were too depleted to care about discipline. Food scarcity after the bombing was only half our problem. Water was the other, or lack of it. St. Bakhita's had only two functioning water boreholes. So instead of getting up every morning for breakfast before class, we were at the boreholes hours before dawn to get water. Just as we had at Kakuma.

Narus had come to a halt. It was not the first time. What I didn't know then was that Narus had been bombed by the government three years earlier. In one attack, a government plane dropped 14 bombs over a period of three days, killing six people, wounding 16. Then I found out that a few months before I arrived, a government plane dropped a dozen bombs on a Catholic mission in Narus, destroying a medical dispensary and injuring six people, including a nurse and five children. The school had been spared in both attacks. That luck could not hold out. And it didn't.

It was April. I had been at the school just under three months. The food scarcity had continued, town donations providing meager provisions spread thin across the student body. I had never been that hungry, not in all the months of fleeing from one village to another staying one step ahead of the government militia, and certainly not in Kakuma where food had been more or less consistent, if not plentiful.

One morning as I sat in class, trying to get my mind off the only thing that mattered, a deafening explosion rocked the building. I held tight to my desk. The whole building shook, windows rattling in sequence like a deck of cards cascading in a line. Glass crashed to the floor—huge pieces blown right inside the classroom. Girls were screaming. Everyone started running outside. It was déjà vu, a replay of the night we fled for our lives in Torit when the government soldiers attacked, the night I got separated from Mom. Bedlam, terror, confusion.

I gathered my wits, following my classmates outside. The air was thick with smoke. In a coughing frenzy, I looked around. It was chaos. No one knew where to run, or if we should run. Rubble littered the grounds. Our teacher appeared, ushering us into the chapel. Nuns did their best to calm the student body, but they seemed as rattled as we were.

After a while when everything was quiet, the teachers dismissed us to our dorms. Later that night we assembled in the dining hall. The nuns informed us that the government had dropped a bomb close to the school. A big one. No students had been badly injured. One girl had been in the bathroom when the bomb hit, the violent blast knocking her to the floor. She was in the infirmary recovering from a sprained ankle and several bruises. Damage to the school was extensive—two buildings near our classroom had been demolished. They would not be operational for some time.

My nerves settled down by nighttime, but I lay wide awake, staring at the ceiling. I could have been in one of the buildings that was demolished. I could easily have been killed. It's a miracle that no one was. In all the time Mom and Likali and Udong and I had wandered the countryside with absolutely no protection, never had I felt as unsafe as I did that night at St. Bakhita's.

Maybe it was because Mom was so far away. Or because the place that was supposed to be safe turned out not to be. Or because every day I woke up wondering if there would be anything to eat. Or because I was so hungry and stressed that I had no emotional strength left. One thing was clear. The nuns could not keep me safe at school any more than Mom could in the wild. And unlike that situation, here Mom could not wrap me in her arms and whisper assurances in my ear. In utter despair, I pulled the cover over my head, then cried myself to sleep. Real wet tears, not the heart kind.

The day of the bombing was a turning point for me. A deep sense of vulnerability lingered long after the event. My concentration faltered. It was difficult to focus on schoolwork. Making matters worse, sleep eluded me, exhausted as I was. Hunger kept me awake, but when I did doze off, the slightest sound would jolt me awake, adrenaline pulsing through me, making it almost impossible to go back to sleep. My already-frail body was wasting away from malnutrition and dehydration, zapping me of whatever energy I might have had to cope. My body and my spirit were tapped out. I began to obsess over the one thing I wanted, the one thing I desperately needed— to go home.

That was not going to happen. Even had the school granted me permission, how would I have gotten there? The hard truth was that I was stuck, captive in a dangerous place far away from everyone I loved. The nightmare of losing Mom when we fled Torit became a recurring flashback. I had vowed that never again would I be separated from my family, and certainly not as a twelve-year-old girl stuck at boarding school, and unsafe one at that.

I slid into a downward spiral that isolated me from everyone, even the girls from home. It didn't matter how many students surrounded me, all I wanted was Mom, and Udong, and Achii. Especially Achii. Any effort I had mustered to fit in with my peers dissipated. There was no point.

In the past, whenever I experienced a low moment at school, the thought of letting Father Elia down boosted my motivation to try harder, and in trying harder I had felt better. This time not only did the thought of letting the priest down fail to motivate me, it felt like pressure. I had enough to do coping with my own depression to care anymore about Father Elia's expectations. His support was inconsequential. I would probably die long before getting out of St. Bakhita's anyway.

Father Elia, my promise to Likali, what did any of it matter. Those dreams and expectations were a fuzzy memory from another lifetime. A lifetime when Mom dug trenches for me and my friends to protect us when bombs fell. A lifetime when I had food in my stomach. A lifetime when I was healthy enough to dream. Now I was going to die, and die in a Catholic boarding school in Narus where belief in St. Bakhita was supposed to give me strength. My childish fantasy of becoming a doctor would die with me.

I knew that even if I survived another close call, this endless war would get me in the end—a random bandit would shoot at the bus going back to Kakuma. Or I would not even get that far, die right here of starvation. Or drink a cup of water infected with Bilharzia, like my sister. There were countless ways I could die at any given moment on any given day. These were the thoughts that consumed me. I became jumpy, agitated. I did not think about the future, only about the next threat.

It wasn't just me. After the bombing, classes and activities started falling apart. Everyone was on edge. Even the adults were preoccupied and nervous. What had been a friendly environment turned hostile overnight. Students became suspicious of one another, alternately defensive and aggressive. Girls broke into arguments over the smallest thing. Patient nuns suddenly began snapping at us. Giggling girls turned silent. Once friendly cliques disintegrated. Teacher enthusiasm was muted. Campus was deserted because no one hung around in casual conversation anymore but scurried to their dorms as if the most important thing after class was to find cover.

You could feel apprehension in the air, a heavy cloud of doom. Walking by the buildings that were now piles of rubble did not help, a constant re-living of that awful day. Everything felt unsettled. I steered clear of any conflict. With my typical low profile, it's likely no one even noticed any difference in my mood or demeanor. Being an introvert had its plusses. Then my luck ran out.

It happened one day in class. I was taking notes in a halfhearted effort to look like I was paying attention, my mind wandering and stomach growling. Out of the blue the girl across from me tapped my arm. Startled, I looked at her. In a harsh whisper, she demanded that I give her my pen. Shaking my head, I returned to my notes. A moment later she pinched my arm, hard, hissing through gritted teeth that she wanted the pen, now. Again, I shook my head and looked down. That's when she hauled off and socked me in the upper arm, the knuckle of her middle finger reaching all the way to my bone with a sharp sting of pain. I jerked my head up, disbelief written all over my face. With her mouth forming a malicious grin, she gingerly extracted the pen from my limp fingers, then batted her eyelashes in sarcastic triumph.

Stunned, all I could do was stare at the girl, who merrily ignored me as the stolen pen flew across her paper. Friends at home had teased me on occasion, but never with meanness. This incident was an assault not only on my being, on my property, but on my dignity as well. The combination of excellent grades and my reserved manner had earned me a degree of respect among the other students. I didn't bother them. They didn't bother me. I was pleasant, friendly, careful not to offend. That strategy had created a bubble, my own little world where I could cope the best I could.

Then just like that, a stolen pen burst the bubble. It might have been a small thing, but it shook me, the unpredictable affront a reflection of how shaky the world had become. Now, in addition to being scared, hungry and lonely, I was jittery, watching my back for the next outburst of anger that might come out of nowhere. In the dorm, I kept my personal belongings hidden from view. In class I kept my head down, one arm curled around my desk as a barrier guarding it.

The incident heightened what had already devolved into an atmosphere brittle with tension. Instead of order that allowed us to focus on schoolwork, a sense of foreboding strained every interaction. Had the nuns been able to assure our safety, they would have. They didn't because they couldn't. In the vacuum of their silence, a collective anxiety took hold, undermining daily life. After the pen incident, it was all I could do to keep up any semblance of academic performance. I no longer cared if my grades fell, or who was disappointed by it. I was twelve years old and no one should ever have expected me to flourish being away from my family.

Other than attending classes, I avoided everyone and anyone unless I absolutely had to speak with them. Then it was a clipped response. My sole focus was to get through each day until enough days passed that I could go home. That was eight months away. One day after maths class, the teacher told me to stay for a minute. When the last student had left the room, he came around from his desk to where I stood. He leaned against the wall, feet crossed in a relaxed position, eyes level with mine. I kept my head down to avoid his gaze.

"Hellen, I can't help wondering what's going on with you. You are my best student in maths, yet lately you don't participate at all, even raise your hand. Your homework is subpar... your overall performance has gone downhill."

My cheeks flushed.

"You don't have to say anything. I'm going to take a wild stab at it. You tell me if I have the facts right."

Shocked by my teacher's concern, I stood motionless, mute, my body stiffened. He spoke in a kind voice.

"The facts are always friendly, don't you think? It might hurt to face them but avoiding them is what causes pain." He tried to make eye contact but failed. "You're a twelve-year-old girl away from your family for the first time, living at a boarding school that two weeks ago was bombed by the Sudanese government."

My heart raced. He continued.

"You're not sleeping well by the look of exhaustion on your face, and your body language. Your stomach is empty. You're frightened. And my guess is that anyone you might turn to right now is far away at home. I'm no genius, Hellen, but I can see you have a lot of stress on those small shoulders." He waited for a response. None came.

"I've been on this earth a lot longer than you, so let me share my wisdom. What you're feeling is normal. You've been through a traumatic experience." I glanced up. He paused. "None of us can stop this war. That I know. Nor can we magically produce a feast. I also know that keeping your feelings inside will not make anything better. In fact, I guarantee that it will make everything worse."

With a shaky breath I met his eyes. He went on.

"The...aggressive girls...are just expressing in their way the same fear and anger and hunger as you. Their way isn't healthy. But your way isn't either. Do you understand?"

"Yes." My voice faltered. I cleared my throat. "Yes."

"Food will find its way to us. The war will come to an end. Until it does, perhaps a little faith in God might be in order."

I nodded with a suppressed smirk. He chuckled softly, as if he got the message that that approach was of no help. His hesitation told me that he wanted to be careful in what he said to a depressed twelve-year-old girl away from home. I could have told him nothing he could say would make me feel worse.

"I know you feel helpless. But you are still the one in charge of your life, Hellen. Not your teachers, not Father Elia. Not your mother. Defeat won't come from outside... like a bomb. But it *will* come if you let it. My bet is that a smart girl like you is not going to let this bad stretch ruin the opportunity you have here at school."

"I won't," I said in an unconvincing tone, still avoiding his gaze.

"No one can tell you what the future holds...whether any of us will be here tomorrow...or ten years from now. But why give up now over a future you cannot predict? You can't control what may or may not happen down the road. The future will come. And when it does, you will face it. In the meantime, you can only live in the present."

I let out a long slow breath, releasing the tension inside.

"You have people who believe in you, Hellen, who believe you will have a better future...in peace, not war.

Why else would they want you to prepare for it?"

For the first time, I made eye contact, staring at him in awe. This man, this teacher, *had* noticed the change in me. He had looked right into my soul, seen my suffering. This was the first time any adult had shown concern since I left Kakuma. All this time I had felt so alone. It had never occurred to me to ask for help from anyone other than Mom. And I would not add to her burden. She needed me to be independent, more grown up than I was. I thought I could, and should, handle this stress alone, like I had all the other times.

On the long dangerous journey to Kakuma, Mom had not been afraid, or if she had, she never let on. I wanted to be like her. Maybe she and my maths teacher had come to the same conclusion that he spoke of now—either we would survive this war, or we would not. But in case we did, the best strategy was to live as if the next day would come. And the next, and the next. That is what my mom had been doing for years. She prepared to keep moving forward. And the days had kept coming. My teacher's voice brought me back to the present.

"You're a brave girl, Hellen, choosing boarding school knowing that it would be almost a year before you could go home. That took courage. But you don't always have to be brave. Technically you're still a child."

This time I did smirk.

"Right. There are no children during war. But there are times when sharing your burden takes more strength than keeping it inside. If we had to walk this earth alone, few would make it, including me. The human species did not survive without helping one another...we're hard wired with empathy for that very reason. No one will think you weak if you let them in every now and then."

I smiled at him, a comfortable, sincere smile of appreciation. That was all the response he needed.

Walking across the yard, I felt lighter, clearer than I had in weeks. How reassuring it was to know that an adult—my maths teacher of all people—had noticed my despair. How odd that another person can see something in you that you had kept inside, and their very acknowledgment of it was a comfort, like you were real. That afternoon I stood at a fork in the road with a decision to make, one that would change me forever.

Why had it suddenly mattered that I felt alone anyway? It seemed I had been on my own all my life, maybe since that terrible night in Torit. Even at four years old, for a fleeting moment, I knew I was going to die, like my friends laying in their own blood at my feet, Mom nowhere in sight. I was totally alone in the horrible chaos of an attack. For those few moments death was in front of me, behind me, all around me. But I didn't die. I went with Imoya. I lived with the terror, survived in the bushes without food or shelter, survived the knowledge that murderous soldiers could appear any moment. And I had done it without my mom, at least for three days. It was clear to me then that I was alone. But something inside me fought to keep going. And when I found Mom everything was alright. Those three days showed me that I could survive anything.

That survival instinct had saved me again at St. Bakhita's. The night we broke into the chicken coop to steal maize, I had decided that I could starve, or I could eat. I had done exactly what my maths teacher said—taken control of my life. Back then I hadn't thought of it that way, but surviving Torit, avoiding starvation, withstanding trauma—terrible things had been happening since I was four. Nothing changed just because I was at St. Bakhita's, only the context was different. School had been such a big dream that part of me wanted to believe it would insulate me from all the bad things happening beyond its walls. It had been a childish fantasy. Safety during wartime was an illusion.

With or without my mother, I had stayed alive. And I hadn't been without her. For years, all my life really, Mom had been teaching me how to survive without her—how to find food when there was none, how to hide from soldiers, how to sleep in the daytime with insects and scorpions surrounded by danger, how to keep going by focusing on the next bush in the distance. Even at St. Bakhita's Mom was telling me what I needed to do. I just hadn't been listening.

My dream of becoming a doctor might never happen for a lot of reasons that had nothing to do with me, things beyond my control. But the only chance it *did* have of happening *was* in my control. Right now it was time to decide. I could go home, and Mom would understand that fear and hunger had become too much to bear. My stomach tightened at what she would think but never say about that decision. I would go back to doing all the things I had done before to help her, help Udong and Achii, not go to school anymore just like most of the other girls. But I also knew for certain that going home would be the end of any dream.

All this time I thought I was so mature. But nothing I had experienced back home had matured me. I was independent. I was capable. I could meet challenges. But now I was facing an obstacle of coping with a circumstance so big and scary that I wanted to run from it. I smiled to myself. I was acting like a little girl. If I wanted to have a grand, grown up dream, then I would need the fortitude to withstand all the bad things that could happen, were happening. And for as long as the war continued, they would keep happening. By the time I reached the dorm, the decision was made. I would prepare for tomorrow and the day after that. I would keep putting one foot in front of the other for however long it took. I would build strength by facing the facts, not hiding from them.

I would believe in God and have hope.

That night I fell into a deep and dreamless sleep. From that day forward I renewed my focus on schoolwork. When classes ended each day, I put in extra hours of study. There was no electricity in the building, but a paraffin lamp in one of the classrooms gave me enough light. In a matter of weeks my performance skyrocketed. Once again, I held top position in every class. My performance was especially noteworthy in maths class. Girls seemed to think it just came naturally to me, that they could not master the material. But they did notice the long hours of study. And they noticed my good grades. Hard work became the blessing that would save me in the future in ways I could not have known at twelve.

What I did know was that day by day the despair that had gripped me cracked, replaced by the deep satisfaction of small successes. My mood improved so much that I actually made an effort to be more outgoing. I made a friend in the process. Stella. Similar in temperament, rather than compete with one another, she and I became something of a team. We studied together, shared notes, quizzed each other before exams. Stella had a big dream too. She wanted to become a teacher at the university level. The chances were miniscule that either of us would achieve our goals. Still, daydreaming with my best friend about a life of success and financial security kept me going. And helped pass the long weekends at school.

When they began rebuilding the dorm that had been demolished by the bomb, Stella and I worked side by side with other students carrying sand and water to the site. We even got paid for it, spending money restoring my position as a capitalist. For the first time at St. Bakhita's, I had fun. Fun!

Later that school year the SPLA captured Kapoeta from government soldiers. The bombing stopped. The fighting stopped. The war ended. A peace agreement was reached and signed by both the north and south, officially ending the Second Sudanese Civil War. It would be six more years before we gained independence as our own country of South Sudan. Life felt almost normal. There would be no more bombs. I relaxed. We all did. When it came time for final exams, the extra study sessions with Stella paid off. I the year with flying colors. Test scores placed me at the top of the class. Stella was right behind me.

For the next eighteen years, I would draw on the strength of one small success after another, remembering my darkest days at St. Bakhita's when one teacher noticed my struggle and made it his business to reach out. My maths teacher will always have a special place in my heart. But there would be others to help me along the way before I got where I was going.

11

HIGH SCHOOL IN NAIROBI
Kenya

Primary school had been a testing ground for me. The long separations from my family forced me to mature in a hurry. In the four years I was at St. Bakhita's, I had four visits home, a month every December for Christmas. It had been difficult, the deep yearning to see Mom, Udong, Achii. But I stayed the course. I was a changed person from the girl who arrived in Narus that dark night four years earlier, the girl who nearly buckled under despair after the bombing.

I was not the only one who had changed. Karoline Achii and John Udong had both grown tall, no longer little kids playing in the dirt. It's funny. At St. Bakhita's, whenever I thought of them, they were the same as the last time I had seen them, frozen, as if everything had moved forward in my world but stood still in theirs. It was always a bit startling to see them after our long separations, not being witness to whatever experiences had resulted in their maturity, only seeing the end result. Whatever adjustments had to be made during my absence, they had made them. Udong and Achii were doing well in school. Mom was the one who worried me.

It turns out she had been suffering from recurring headaches, which finally drove her to seek treatment at the Kakuma clinic. High blood pressure, that is what the nurse told her. By the time I came home from St. Bakhita's, the medication was helping. Still, Mom's energy level seemed low. It did not occur to me that aging might be a factor. I may have grown older, Udong and Achii along with me, but Mom was our immortal matriarch. She was still the same capable, strong woman she had been four years ago, but she had slowed a step. Udong and Achii had become more helpful than I ever remembered, a blessing for Mom. Less guilt for me.

When she asked about school, I recounted the good parts, the achievements. Everything else I kept to myself—the depression, especially after the bombing, which I also left out, and the endless hunger. As I look back, I wonder if Mom saw me the way I saw her—undaunted by life's challenges. Or maybe she kept as much from me as I did from her. Mom would not have shared her burdens with a child, but I was quite grown up now. That did not matter.

Mom and I had established a pattern early on. Even as I was about to start high school, nothing changed between us. She still did not confide in me. When my maths teacher encouraged me to share with someone if my burden got too heavy, I knew that someone would never be my mother. We were two stoic women, each keeping our own counsel. If anyone understood that the facts were friendly, it was Mom, facing reality head-on, no matter how hard the truth. And those truths had been brutal. I thought about the look on her face during our long journey when the soldier told her my father was not at the new SPLA headquarters, that no one knew where he was. All those months before we reached Kakuma she had no way of knowing if he was dead or alive until he showed up that first year at the camp. Yet if Mom had been distressed, she never let on to us kids. On some level I had always known that she expected the same of me. And so my anxiety about starting high school in a new country where everyone would be a stranger—that I kept to myself.

In January of 2005 after Christmas holiday, I began the next phase of my education as a high school student in Nairobi. Saying goodbye to Mom, my dear Achii and Udong had become a bittersweet ritual after four years of my single annual visits. All of us held our emotions in check at what would be another months-long sepa-ration. My stomach was in knots. Of the five of us girls who had left together for St. Bakhita's four years earlier, I was the only one going on to high school, thanks to the continued support from Father Elia. Akera and Betty had dropped out of St. Bakhita's in their third year. The two sisters had been taken by their brother to study in a town called Eldoret, a big city in the Rift Valley region of Kenya. I was the only one heading to high school in Nairobi.

It was always a mystery to me how a Catholic priest could afford to support the education of five girls. Father Elia's salary from the Church would not have made him wealthy. In choosing the five of us, perhaps he had anticipated exactly what happened, that not all of us would finish, making ongoing support of whichever ones did that much more feasible. Though I admitted feeling bad about the others, I also felt proud about keeping my word. I had not disappointed the guardian of my future who had believed in me from the start. He seemed proud of me too. *You just do your part, Hellen. Let me and God worry about the rest.* Father Elia, along with my maths teacher, had become the pillars of belief in my ability to succeed. That was the thought sustaining me as I boarded the bus that January afternoon bound for Nairobi.

When the five of us from Kakuma had left for St. Bakhita's, making our way to Narus sixteen miles away, that was one thing. The short distance had been difficult enough. Traveling to a big city in a neighboring country was a level of challenge Father Elia saved me from taking on alone. To my great relief, he had arranged for a middle-aged woman named Elizabeth, also on her way to Nairobi, to accompany me.

Elizabeth saved me the seat next to her, a box of snacks for the two of us in her lap. The trip to Nairobi would take a full twenty-four hours. After a while on the road, the bus fell quiet, most everyone lulled to sleep by the gentle rhythm. I was too nervous to sleep. Out the window, the barren wasteland of Kakuma gave way to the forested landscape of Kenya, sliding by in fast-forward motion into the night. The rocking of the bus had a hypnotic effect, pulling me into a melancholy hole. Loneliness, the one emotion I battled most, pressed against my chest, the vast emptiness outside magnifying my smallness. Other than Kakuma, which was on the border with Kenya, I had never been out of southern Sudan. St. Bakhita's had been its own world, our only contact with Narus the annual transport home. Nairobi was a huge metropolis. In another country.

It was not as if I were a backward tribal girl steeped in traditions of my ancestors. We had changed with the times like other tribes, adapted to a world of global communication connected by the internet. Still, at heart I was a country girl, and the idea of a sprawling city with hundreds of thousands of people, rapid transit and skyscrapers did feel daunting. I was sixteen years old, but on that bus, I was twelve again, alone in the world.

Nairobi, Kenya

Classes at Stonebic High School in Form 1 were not much harder than my final year at St. Bakhita's. By the time I got to Form 2 in 2006, the course work was a bit more challenging, which was fine with me. Science came easy to me with all my extra studying, or over studying. Everyone in my science class, including the teacher, was astonished that I knew the finer points of the Krebs Cycle, untangling which step in the process carbon dioxide molecules were formed. Awed at my test scores, students and teachers soon came to respect the work habits that kept me at the top of the class from day one. In high school, just as it had been in primary school, I was acutely aware of Father Elia's investment in me. Only now the discipline that had yielded success had become a part of me. The pressure was internal, belief in myself pushing me to succeed. *Defeat won't come from outside, Hellen.*

August of that year turned out to be the coldest on record. In class everyone wrapped up in jackets, hands either tucked inside or underneath us for warmth. One afternoon, during our last class of the day, it was so cold that students were fidgety. I struggled to stay focused, trying to figure out how to keep my hands warm under me and write at the same time. Biology was my favorite subject, which helped on such a bitter afternoon. I had finished the worksheet and was glancing over our homework assignment when the school secretary entered the classroom. She approached the teacher, whispering into his ear. We all looked up to see what was going on, a welcome distraction from the cold. The secretary then stood by the door and waited. My teacher motioned me to his desk. I was to go with her to the headmistress's office. Bewildered, I glanced back at my papers, then left the room.

In the cold drizzle I trotted behind her, my mind drawing a complete blank as to why the headmistress would want to see me. Then it dawned on me. As deputy head girl, I had responsibilities that required me to speak with the headmistress from time to time. Relieved, I followed the secretary into the office, which felt almost as cold as outside. The headmistress sat at her desk with two visitors, a man and a woman, sitting across from her. A third chair was empty.

I did not recognize the woman. The man was a friend of Father Elia's, Father Matthew. I recognized him right away. The two priests had visited me at school. I smiled a greeting. He stood up, his reply a subdued nod of acknowledgement, his face somber. Then I noticed the others looked somber too—the headmistress, the secretary, the woman visitor, whose name was Veronica something. My stomach turned.

"Have a seat, Hellen," the headmistress said.

From the tone of her voice, an undercurrent of concern, I knew this had nothing to do with my role as deputy head girl. Father Matthew motioned toward the empty chair across from his. I stared at it tentatively, as if the cushion might have nails. I perched on the edge. Father Matthew cleared his throat and leaned forward, elbows on his knees.

"Hellen, I...well, I have some bad news for you I'm afraid." My breath stopped. He shifted in the chair. "My dear girl, I am so sorry to tell you, but..."

"What? What's happened?"

"It's Father Elia. He...well, it was very sudden...but...he died this morning."

The room spun. I watched the scene from above, floating weightlessly. The woman visitor said something to me. It was too garbled to make out, as if she had pebbles in her mouth. A buzzing in my head got louder. I fell back in the chair. *Father Elia...dead? How can that be possible?* There must be some mistake. I tried to process the news.

I stared at Father Matthew. "Are you sure?"

"Quite sure." He let out a deep sigh.

The buzzing noise in my head stopped. The room stopped spinning. I stared out the window, soft drizzle making the glass blurry, like my mind. I sat there, lost in disbelief at an announcement that made no sense. *This cannot be true.* Someone was speaking to me.

"Hellen." The headmistress called my name. "Hellen." I turned to her, mute, confused. "Father Matthew would like you to go with him. I'll make sure your books get to the dorm safely."

In a daze I followed the priest down the hallway out to his car, too stunned to ask where we were going. Half an hour later the two of us stood in the lobby of the hospital where Father Elia had died that morning. Father Matthew gently took my arm and led me into the elevator. He pushed the Down button. The doors opened once, but he pressed Down again.

When the elevator opened again, we stood facing steel gray doors. DEPARTMENT OF THE MEDICAL EXAMINER-COR-ONER. My feet refused to move. Father Matthew put one arm around my shoulder as he pushed through the double doors. The smell of antiseptic broke my trance. This was no dream, no out-of-body experience. In robotic movements, I walked to a gurney. Father Elia's lifeless body lay peacefully draped in a white cloth up to his shoulders. His face was pale, the bluish white of death. I knew that color because I had seen it before—on Likali.

In his prone position the priest looked almost young, his frown lines and smile lines etched in tiny squiggles instead of rivulets. He could've been asleep, his demeanor belying the trauma of death. The last time I saw him, only a week earlier, he had been full of energy, purpose. A million things to do on his goodwill mission between Narus and Nairobi. How could he be dead? Of all the awful unforeseen things that had happened in my life, and the ones I imagined might, Father Elia's death was not remotely among them.

My knees began to quiver. A shudder ran through me. From somewhere deep inside a guttural, anguished cry broke the silence. I clasped my hands over my ears, shut my eyes, refusing to accept the devastating truth. Father Matthew took me by the shoulders to a chair before I collapsed. My whole body shook, every pent-up emotion gushing out in a torrent of pain. I don't know how long I sat there crying. I don't remember Father Matthew being there. I don't remember leaving the morgue.

The next thing I knew, Father Matthew was driving, Veronica in the passenger seat. The world whizzed by as if everything were normal, the windshield wipers beating in rhythm like a metronome. Father Matthew kept checking on me in the rearview mirror as I sat in a stupor. Instead of returning to school, he drove to the woman's home. Father Matthew said something to me, something to her, then he was gone.

I ate the porridge Veronica put in front of me. The woman did not say anything. When I finished, she led me to a small room she had made up, then left. I dropped on the bed, staring at the ceiling. An hour ago, I had been sitting in biology class, my major problem figuring out which homework subject to start on after school. In the short time between then and now, between stability and chaos, the known and unknown, everything had changed. Father Elia, gone. In all the times I had felt alone the last five years, I always knew he was somewhere in the background. I had never asked him for help, but I knew he would have given it had I asked.

What now? What would happen to me? All the talk about education being the road to a better life had just hit a dead end. Father Elia as my benefactor had been the one holding everything up, making school possible, this dear man who had been an unfaltering source of hope that extended far beyond his confidence in me. He was a priest, a man of God. I believed he was all-powerful, invincible, that all I had to do to succeed was my part. *Let me and God take care of the rest, Hellen.*

Now everything was gone, any hope of becoming a doctor laying alongside Father Elia in the morgue. It wasn't just the financial support, the belief in me. Until that moment I had not grasped how strong the bond that held me to him, an umbilical cord of nutrients sustaining me with belief, support. A future. No father could have done more to shape me into the person I had become these last five years.

My own father had been out of my life since Torit, except for the two visits at Kakuma, the second one to celebrate Achii's birth nine months after the first one. That was ten years ago. That loss had taken the form of a dull ache, a hole in my heart from what I did not get from my father, with my father. Love, affection, concern, knowledge. Father Elia had been more real to me than my own dad, the memory of him faded with time. He loved me. I knew that. But we had not been a family since I was one year old the night when he was captured by SPLA soldiers in Lafon. My love for him was more theoretical than real, patched together from a few small memories of being happy with him, precious moments with all of us together.

With Father Elia's death I had lost the most important man in my life. Mom had always been there for me, always would be. But Mom didn't know the world beyond Kakuma, know the enormity, the intensity of my dream, nor the obstacles I had to clear every step of the way. That was my doing. As long as Father Elia understood what I faced, what I had to do to succeed, that was enough.

At least I had gotten this far. I had to wonder if my success at school brought him joy. It must have, knowing his sponsorship would ensure that my life would be different from my mother's, different from ninety-nine percent of girls in Sudan. Like a loving parent, Father Elia had put me on the path to financial stability in adulthood, a way to live in relative safety with the means to help my family. Only a man of God could pull that off in the middle of a bloody war. While most in my generation faced a bleak future in the poverty of displacement, I did not. Or had not until now. Now that everything was gone.

Those first few days after Father Elia's death I was inconsolable, pulled under in the quicksand of loss, unable to breathe or grab hold of anything to stop the descent into total despair. Then, as it had with Likali, despair twirled into anger. What a cruel world. There was no point in praying. Father Elia had abandoned me.

It was a selfish thought, but I didn't care. His death was desertion as sure as my own father's exit from our lives. Like any child, I had accepted that reality. But I never stopped wishing my dad would come back. Until that day in church when Father Elia showed up and heard me sing. Now I had lost my father all over again.

Father Elia's body was transported to southern Sudan for burial. I was still at Veronica's lost in grief. Ten days later, Father Mathew visited. We sat outside in the shade. I wasn't much in the mood for talking. He didn't push. For a while we just sat. Finally Father Matthew reached into his pocket. He pulled out a piece of paper.

"I have something for you." He nodded for me to go ahead and read it. The note was from Father Elia. My heart caught in my throat.

"Agwak, I want you to continue your education by all means."

Stunned, I looked at Father Matthew, then read the note again. It was the shortest message I had ever received in writing. I had no idea how a girl of sixteen was supposed to come up with those means. My spirit was so depleted that any inspiration I might have had was not forthcoming. In the meantime, I returned to school to await arrangements for transportation home from Nairobi. My mind had been dulled since Father Elia's death, a veil of sorrow dimming my view of everything, making any great revelation unlikely about how I was supposed to move forward. One thing was clear, there would be plenty of time to think about it at home. The thought of starting over was too awful to consider. How likely was it that there was another Father Elia in my future?

Two weeks later, I was summoned to the headmistress's office again, the memory of that awful day breaking through as I walked across the yard. Father Matthew was there, sitting exactly where he had been that day. He was the only visitor. This time the headmistress left the room. Father Matthew smiled, motioning me to sit down.

"This time I have good news, Hellen."

I managed a weak smile, my body heavy in the chair. Unless he had arranged for Father Elia to be resurrected, it was hard to imagine what news that could be.

Father Matthew chuckled. "Okay. Since you're not asking, I'll go ahead and tell you." His eyes twinkled. "I've met with the school administration. Along with me, the school will pay your fees for the remaining part of Form 2."

My mouth dropped open.

He grinned. "Not only that...we will provide an allowance...for incidentals and such." He leaned back, letting the words sink in. I smiled at the priest.

Just like that, my future had a path forward. Father Elia was still looking after me. Once the euphoria wore off that my education wasn't dead in the water, the inevitable reality returned. What would happen after Form 2. The uncertainty of how I would go on after that returned like an old friend back from vacation. When all had been lost, the constant buzzing of anxiety in my head stopped. Futility was quiet. But now there was hope. The buzzing of anxiety returned. I decided to take the advice of my maths teacher not to worry about a future I could not predict. I would live as if I expected tomorrow to come. Father Elia and Father Matthew had dropped down from heaven right in my path. It was sheer fantasy to expect that a third angel would simply appear with the answer. I may not have been able to predict the future, but at least mine was back on the table. For now. That would have to be enough. I had renewed my commitment to find the funds somewhere. I had come this far, and no way was I giving up now. In the meantime, I had fallen behind in my classes. There was plenty of work to do.

12

OUT OF DARKNESS

Nairobi

As the end of Form 2 drew near, the buzzing returned as anxiety about Form 3 took hold. I struggled to stay optimistic. Crossing the quad one afternoon a notice caught my eye. In two days, a meeting was scheduled about educational support for South Sudanese students. Those in good academic standing who lacked funds to continue high school might qualify. The discussion would be led by a boy from the Dinka tribe—one of the Lost Boys who had made it to Kakuma Refugee Camp, boys orphaned when their villages were attacked. They had covered southern Sudan on foot, walking over a thousand miles for two years in search of safety before they were found and taken to Kakuma. One of those survivors was a man named Mariel. He would be our speaker.

Two days later in the assembly hall, five of us sat fidgeting with anticipation. I was one of three girls. When the meeting began, a member of the school board spoke first. I was so anxious to hear about the financial aid that I could hardly listen. Then it was Mariel's turn to speak. A majestic looking man, he sounded educated, his Dinka height adding a quiet authority to his kind demeanor. Mariel started with his own story. The room fell silent. We already knew the story of these Lost Boys but hearing about the experience firsthand was chilling. One of only half who survived, Mariel's story had a good ending. At that time, the United States was accepting refugees who were sponsored by someone in the U.S. Churches and non-profits worked finding families who volunteered to take in an orphaned boy. Mariel was one of the chosen few. CNN even made a documentary about them. That sponsorship program ended when the TV show faded from memory, by which time the sheer number of refugees had taken its toll on the good will of the United States government.

The five of us listened, spellbound by Mariel's tragic story and eventual success. I was especially captivated, thinking about my own journey, unable to imagine how I would have fared on my own at six, the age of many of the boys. When he finished, Mariel explained that he was at Stonebic representing a program that had been established to help any high school students struggling to pay school fees. Especially girls. He paused, then looked right at me. My mouth dropped open—*especially girls.* As if on cue, the three of us looked at each other in awe. Mariel finished the talk saying he was available to anyone interested in applying.

The screech of chairs filled the room as we pulled closer to Mariel, forming a semicircle. Then each of us in turn explained our situation. Mariel listened without interruption. Then he told us more about the foundation sponsoring bright students in need of financial support. A man named Mr. Ken managed the program. He was the one who would review all applications and make the final determination of which student or students qualified. Mariel's job was to identify those potential recipients.

In a group reflex, we all sat up straight. Mariel looked at each of us in turn, rubbing his chin like a professor contemplating the universe. He leaned forward and handed an application to the boy at the end of the row. A small grin emerged on Mariel's face. He sat back eyeing each one of us, again rubbing his chin in deep thought. Then he handed an application to the next boy. My shoulders slumped. I stared at my shoes to hide the disappointment that was surely on my face. A white form appeared under my nose. An application. I looked up to see Mariel grinning. He had given one to each of us!

Murmurs of joy and relief buzzed through our group. Mariel reached out his hands, palms down, as if patting a bed to test its softness. We quieted. His face was serious as he described our task—to collect previous school transcripts along with the fee structures and send those documents with the completed application form. Within a month we would have an answer. It would be the slowest month of my life.

I got right to work mailing St. Bakhita's for my transcripts. The registrar at Stonebic gathered my Form 1 and

Form 2 records to date. He placed all my documents in a big manila envelope and stamped it. Then the wait began. Each day I marked the calendar, the number of days shrinking as slow as sorghum molasses.

Three weeks later I was studying on my bed. There was a knock on the door. It was too soon. But there was a phone call for me in the dorm office. Who would be calling me? Taking the stairs two at a time, I grabbed the receiver in both my shaking hands.

"Is this Hellen Onyango I'm speaking with?"

"Yes, Sir."

"Well, Miss Onyango, this is Mr. Ken from the foundation for financial assistance that Mariel came to your school and spoke about. I've had a chance to review your application." He paused. My heart stopped. "It is my pleasure to inform you that we have awarded you a scholarship to cover fees for both Forms 3 and 4. You're going to finish high school."

I was mute.

"Miss Onyango...Hellen...are you there?"

"Yes...yes, Sir. Thank you very much. I won't let you down."

A soft chuckle came through. "No...I don't think you will. Yours was the first application packet to reach our office. If your initiative in pursuing this scholarship—tracking down the documents, getting them posted—is any measure of your motivation, then our money will be well spent."

"Thank you, Sir."

"You're exactly the kind of student we need who can finish high school, go on to university. It's students like you who will contribute to the wellbeing of our country."

"Yes, Sir." I was back in Kakuma, hearing Father Elia's words all over again.

"You're already well versed in the kinds of obstacles girls face getting an education. It seems so far you haven't been daunted enough to quit."

"No, Sir." I rolled my eyes, wondering if I sounded as much like the idiot I felt like at the moment.

"We believe you can go the distance, Hellen. South Sudan needs you."

"Yes, Sir."

"Well...it was nice chatting with you. I like to speak personally to all our recipients. You'll be getting a packet of information in the post, as will the registrar."

"Thank you, Sir."

I think he chuckled again before ending the call, or maybe I'm mistaken. It didn't matter. I took the stairs slowly on my way back, smiling up to the heavens. "Thank you, Father Elia."

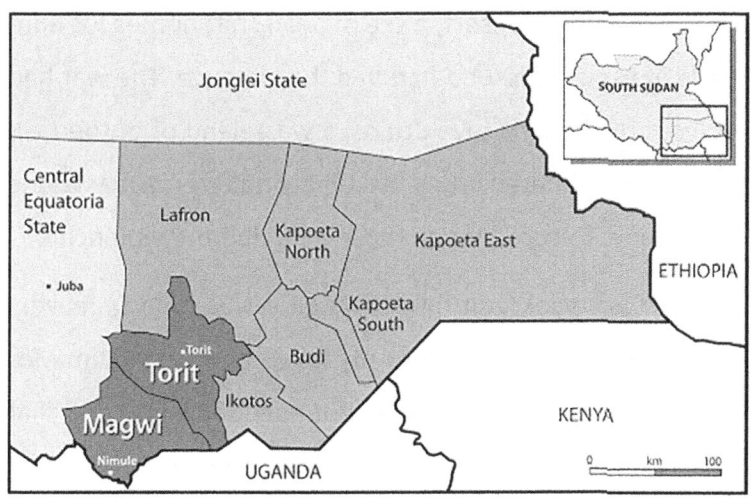

LAFON, EASTERN EQUITORIA, SOUTHERN SUDAN

I graduated from Stonebic High School in December 2008 and returned to South Sudan, but not before stopping in Kakuma to visit my family. They were enormously proud of me for my accomplishments, and they never even knew the hard part. Being in Kakuma, seeing my friends, I felt more isolated than ever. The gift of education had also taken me further from the refugee life I might have had without Father Elia. After living in Nairobi, Kakuma seemed small. And I had never felt more out of place.

Kakuma had always seemed big to me. In the decade since we arrived it had grown exponentially, sprawling across the barren desert, a sea of makeshift homes for hundreds of thousands who had fled the violence. The war had ended, but the land lay in ruins, a wasteland of burned villages and decimated crops. Kakuma would remain as home in the years to come for all those who fled the violence.

Our two-week visit flew by, then it was time to leave. I had been saying goodbye to my loved ones in Kakuma for eight years. It never got easier. But I needed a job, and that meant going to Torit. The midday sun beat down on the car as I drove through Narus—the once-gaping distance between home and St. Bakhita's diminished by road improvements and the end of war. I passed through Kapoeta, the village where Mom and I had stayed after fleeing Torit and walking to Nimule. I pulled the sun visor down to block the glare. So many memories crossed my mind driving through this area, visions of being on foot caught somewhere between living and dying. During the school term I had been so focused on my studies that I never thought about the past. Driving long hours on the open road with my mind free, the memories came flooding back as if they had happened yesterday.

As I reached the outskirts of Torit, the city looked completely unfamiliar. I remembered being happy here as a little girl there, oblivious to what lay ahead the awful night we fled for our lives. But the outskirts of town showed no evidence of our lives there. The town was bustling. I had no problem finding a place to stay.

My search began first thing the next morning. Scouring the paper, I spotted an ad—a Norwegian Church providing humanitarian aid needed a health educator. The ad had just been placed that morning. I called to schedule an interview. Twenty-four hours later, I was employed.

That news had been good enough, but my mouth dropped open when they told me where I would be working—Lafon! Wouldn't Mom be happy about that! All the stories she had told me about life with my father, how he loved his farming and cattle herding, how happy she had been as a new wife and mother, how Grandma wouldn't leave with us when we had to flee. That part of my history was short, but precious. If you were to draw a pie chart of my life with sections divided by years of happiness, Lafon would make up the narrowest slice. But it would be the sweetest, visions of a happy family passed down from my mother to be stored away. Someday I would have a family of my own. When South Sudan was at peace.

Hellen Onyango, M.D., 2020

Elated to be employed, I left Torit for the health facility in Lafon in a rented car with two men who had also been hired as health educators. I was relieved at having landed a job so soon, puffed with pride at the prospect of making real money for the first time in my life, excluding my jaunt as a construction worker alongside Stella at St. Bakhita's carrying sand and water to the building site of the new dorm for spending money.

A real job meant I would be able to help Mom. The employment package was not that much, but good for a high school graduate. The larger significance was that it was a health-related job, the first line of a resume´ that would end with the letters 'M.D.' That was still years away, but unlike other phases of my education, this would become part of the patchwork of experience I would accumulate on the way. Who knew how long it would be before I made it to medical school? Or any higher education, the state system in shambles after two decades of war. But time was relative, one thing I had learned during years of displacement. The pressure of accomplishing X by this age or Y by that age had lost all meaning. However long it took, I would get there. Of that I had no doubt.

Maybe I would have to be escorted out of med school in a wheelchair, but I would earn those two letters after my name.

First things first. As a health educator in Lafon my job would be to teach basic public health measures—prevention, especially for diseases easily transmissible in close living quarters. Hygiene and sanitation seemed like common sense practices, but some households had major obstacles to overcome, access to water one. Dysentery-like diseases could spread like wildfire, and kill with dehydration, like it had with my sister. And I would emphasize that washing hands after using the toilet and before eating was a particularly effective way to break the chain of transmission of disease-causing bacteria. I was so ready to be a great educator.

Once people understood the theory, new awareness would be the first step in behavior change. I had absolute confidence in my skills. The community would develop healthy habits in no time. That was my thinking when I first arrived in Lafon, weeks before I realized that changing habits for an entire community was like pushing a barrel of rocks uphill. No matter. I was full of energy and enthusiasm.

As our car approached the clinic, children appeared out of nowhere, running behind our car, squealing with excitement at visitors. The hearty welcome reassured us that people would be open to teaching from a stranger. My having been born in their village wouldn't hurt my credibility either. Most of the children were naked, some with tattered clothes that probably had not been washed in weeks, laden with who-knows-what contaminants.

But as a general assessment the children looked healthy. Naked or partially clothed, dirty and oblivious— they were just normal kids. Had I been born in another time my childhood in Lafon might have looked just like theirs. How odd that I had come full circle to the very place it all started.

Photos courtesy of Kenneth Waxman, M.D.

The Church had set up a mini dorm for the three of us in one of the classrooms no longer in use. The rooms were covered in dust. As I cleaned my area, a yell from one of the guys got my attention. Peeking through the open door between our rooms, I watched as both of them scrambled near one of the beds. On the floor beneath it a snake slithered this way and that, as if he were just as confused and frightened having been disturbed as the guys were in finding it there. It took some maneuvering, but between the two of them, they managed to nudge the creature out the door. I smiled to myself. Clearly neither of them had ever lived in the bushes. Maybe I would tell them about waking up face to face with a giant scorpion.

The next morning, we started work. As I walked around the village it soon became obvious that basic health education might be easy to teach, but hard to implement. Plumbing had not made its way to Lafon. Home after home had no toilet. Even in public places there were none. Adults and children alike were defecating in the bushes close to where they lived, the perimeter of the village essentially an open latrine. There was no social stigma associated with the practice, just as there was none going naked. The Pari had been the last villagers to be attacked by the outside world. Some practices associated with our ancient way of life were still the norm.

Even had the norm been different, poverty dictated that people make do with what they had, the basic rule of survival. All of South Sudan struggled after the war given the ongoing conflict between the Dinka and Nuer over control of our young country. Luckily, I had only Lafon to worry about. It would be a challenge of creative innovation teaching hygiene practices without the benefit of soap and clean water.

I began pushing the barrel of rocks uphill.

Soap and water turned out to be the least of it, dashing my assumption that education would lead directly to behavior change. People did not believe the most powerful prevention for dysentery-like diseases was simple hand washing. No magic. No medicine. No doctor or nurse needed. Soap would be ideal, of course, but even without soap the friction from rubbing your hands in water would do the trick. It was easy enough to teach.

Except no one believed me. This was the moment I realized I had the perfect temperament for public health—

chronic intractable problems rather than one-time fixes. Slow progress. Nothing dramatic. That was okay. My real strength lay in patience. Nothing in my life had come easily or quickly. Working in public health would be like everything else I had undertaken, success achieved one step at a time day in and day out, not looking up at the mountain ahead but clearing the blocked road moving one pebble at a time. The challenge for me would be not to get discouraged, not to look for progress in big chunks, but in tiny increments. Slow I could do. Slow I had been doing all my life. I had learned a thing or two about persistence and was not easily daunted by the size of a task or the noise of a ticking clock.

Three years into my job, I met an older South Sudanese man who was also from Lafon. Doctor Hilary had been practicing in Italy for two decades. He was impressed that I had finished high school, 'an extraordinary accomplishment for a girl,' is what he called it. We enjoyed long talks about this and that—medical practice, the war, the future of healthcare in South Sudan. Dr. Hilary had returned to Lafon to visit and work for a few months. He would not be staying.

I was disappointed. He was the first person who really understood my dream, had lived it, could see my determination. How I would miss him. It was a few days before he left when we finished our work at the clinic. We walked outside together, chatting easily. A few minutes later he stopped, pausing for a moment before saying he had a story to tell me. We sat on a bench in the shade. Like Father Elia had been to me, Dr. Hilary had well-wishers who had seen promise in him. Those kind souls had sponsored his education.

My shoulders slumped, as they always did at the topic of how to fund the next leg of my education. My mastery of living in the present was not the greatest, worry about money always with me. Dr. Hilary stopped talking, waiting for my attention to return from its wandering.

He smiled. "Hellen, if you have come this far, it's because people have believed in you, wanted to help. You have faced unbelievable obstacles and somehow not only managed to overcome them, but stayed at the top of your classes while doing it! That tells me everything I need to know. You are going to make it all the way. And I would like to help you do that...offer you the same support others have given me, sort of a way of paying it forward."

I stared at the man, too dumbstruck to say anything. Doctor Hilary chuckled. "I'll take that as a 'yes.'"

"This is an unbelievable gift. How can I ever thank you?"

"That's easy. Someday you'll be a doctor. Maybe there will be someone out there who has a dream but needs help. A girl even." He grinned. It was the same big smile Father Elia had, the same one as Father Matthew, the same lilt in his voice as that of Mr. Ken from the financial aid foundation that helped me pay for Stonebic.

It was May of 2011 when I handed in my resignation at the clinic and headed back to Nairobi. I would be starting pre-med at Mount Kenya University in three weeks. I was really on my way.

Two months later, in July of 2011, southern Sudan became the youngest country in the world—The Republic of South Sudan. Together we stood on the precipice of a promising future.

Nyal

Me at University of Kenya Medical School

13

CHASING DOWN A DREAM

Nairobi, Kenya

My journey to Nairobi took longer than I had intended. The time gap between leaving the Lafon clinic and starting university in pre-med would probably be the only opportunity I would have for a long time to do something that had been on my mind for years. I returned to Torit on the way back to Kakuma. I had no idea where my father had been buried. Someone told me a local couple had known him, maybe they could direct me. But they had no idea either.

All they could tell me was the cause of death—malaria. He had survived life as a soldier, the horrors of civil war, only to die from the bite of a mosquito, like so many of our countrymen and women who managed to survive terrible hardships in their lives, taken down by a flying insect. The irony was bitter. But I needed to hear it, to know how my father died. After walking around town for a while, thinking about the two years Mom and I had spent waiting for the war to end, waiting for my father to make us a family again, waiting, waiting, waiting, I said goodbye to Torit, to the place where my father had lived his life without us after we fled the attack, spent his final days and had been laid to rest.

I arrived at Kakuma in the late afternoon, eager to see Mom, Udong and Achii, both teenagers, nearly full grown. Imagine my surprise at meeting two new members of the family. A year earlier my mom had traveled back to South Sudan to retrieve the children of my father's second wife in Nimule where she moved after his death. The woman could no longer care for them. My father was finally with us, after so many years, in the person of Susan Akoo, who was eight, and little Moses Anur, six years old, an infant when my father died.

There were two more mouths to feed, but Mom, still working as a cook for an NGO, looked happy to have them, fussing over little kids again. Achii and Udong were equally enthralled with their new siblings, Achii immediately taking on the role of bossy big sister, Udong happy to be a big brother. As always when I visited home, Likali's spirit filled the place. In meeting little Moses, I finally saw myself at that age, a six-year-old girl trying to save my sister. The impossibility of such a task lightened some of my intractable guilt.

I had two weeks to get to Nairobi to start school. Problems arranging transportation to Kenya stalled me. Worried about missing my first classes at university, I retrieved enough money to buy a bus ticket from what I had given Mom. It felt like serendipity when I boarded that bus to Nairobi, the same one I had taken seven years earlier on my way to Stonebic High.

The snag in transportation meant I arrived at university two weeks late. The woman in administration assured me the school hostel was still mine. She also gave me contact information so I could email my professors. It was late afternoon when I got to my room. I would be sharing with three other girls. Two double beds took up most of the space. It would be a tight squeeze, four women living together. The bathrooms were a distance from the hostels, but that small inconvenience hardly registered in my thrill at being there.

That evening I met two of my roommates, the giggly sort I remembered from St. Bakhita's. But they were in pre-med like me, so they must have been serious students. As night fell, my long journey caught up with me. I needed sleep. The two girls took up both beds with their loud music and giggles. They took no notice of my not-so-subtle cues, big yawns, stretching arms. After a while it was clear they intended to ignore me. I curled up in the chair, turned toward the wall, my back to them, convinced the partying would wind down at some point.

No such luck. A light tap at the door marked the arrival of two boys met by gleeful giggles from my roommates. The men's hostel was about 200 meters from ours, so it made sense that we would have a lot of contact with a shared kitchen and dining hall. But late-night visitors seemed unusual. This was not a coed dorm. No one in the room took any notice of me, scrunched up in the chair, sweater over my head to block the noise. The partying continued for hours. By two in the morning there was no sign of anyone going anywhere, including me to bed, which was now occupied by one couple, the other couple in what should have been my bed. I dozed on and off in what passed for sleep. Between irritation at their lack of consideration for my presence, and utter embarrassment, it was an extremely uncomfortable night.

By daybreak the guys were gone. Roommates still asleep, I gathered my things. After washing up, I went directly to class. If these girls were any measure of life here, it would be a very lonely four years. In the meantime, I was a wreck from lack of sleep, not an ideal state of mind for my first day of university. Mr. Buya was the head of our Life Science department. I met him at his office as instructed so he could escort me to my first class—anatomy. It was already in session when Mr. Buya introduced me to the lecturer and students. Already behind, I prayed the material would not be too challenging. Sleep-deprivation, along with a sense of disorientation that comes with being in unfamiliar surroundings, I was not at my best.

The lecturer motioned me to take a desk next to a girl named Daphny. She smiled at me by way of introduction. The material was not totally foreign. Trying to get my bearings, I half listened while scouring the textbook to see what had already been covered. My shoulders tensed when the lecturer announced that we would have a continuous assessment test on Friday, two days away! Sitting alone after class was dismissed, I slumped in the desk, trying to come up with a strategy for catching up in two short days. There was no way I was going to fail my first test in university. The lecturer had no office hours that day. I would have to figure it out on my own. I let out an exasperated sigh at my predicament. How would I feel explaining to Dr. Hilary that I had already botched pre-med? My whole life had been in preparation for this moment.

"It's Hellen...right?"

Startled, I sat up straight. Daphny was standing next to the desk, smiling. She dropped into the seat across the aisle and faced me. She must have read my face.

"Look, don't worry, you'll catch up. I can help. I have classes the rest of the day, but why don't you meet me later this evening in the library. We can go over what you've missed. By tomorrow you'll be caught up."

I shook my head slightly in disbelief and smiled. "Thank you. I really appreciate that." I gathered my books, reflecting on my great good luck in sitting down next to Daphny. As I made my way to Physiology, it occurred to me that in all my years of school, never had anyone been so nice so fast. Tired as I was, my step had a bounce. The rest of the day went smoothly, buoyed by knowing that help was on the way.

In the evening I met Daphny in the library. We took a table near the back so we could speak without disturbing others. She opened her book to what they had covered in class the previous two weeks—introduction to cells, tissue and organs.

Relief surged through me. This was more review than new material, information included in my high school biology class, though not with the level of detail. Daphny and I discussed what might be on the test and reviewed some of the content, enough that I had some sense of where to focus. Daphny again offered a helping hand when she suggested we meet for the next two days, study together until the test. The memory of Stella and our marathon study sessions popped into my head, our strategy for getting through long weekends at St. Bakhita's when the locals went home.

Walking back to the hostels with Daphny, I mentioned the previous night, the boys sleeping in our room, and asked if that was allowed. An emphatic 'no' was her response. But she confessed that sleeping together was a common occurrence, though most of the time the girls went to the boys' hostel. We laughed crossing the campus, conjuring disastrous scenes of boys escaping in the dead of night.

What had started out as a terrible first day ended on a high note. Daphny's support was meaningful not only because of the exam, but because I had made a friend, a friend who would ease the loneliness that continually shadowed me. I did not know it then, but Daphny would become my closest friend as we went through university and then medical school together. Now a physician at a hospital in Mombasa, our bond continues to this day.

True to his word, Dr. Hilary sponsored my education. It was hard to believe my good fortune at being free of the anxiety that had plagued me since the day Father Elia died. It was 2015 with one year of med school left to go that I hit a bump. Dr. Hilary's growing financial constraints prevented him from ongoing support. I did not collapse with despair. There had to be a way. I was determined to find it.

Scouring the Internet for scholarship sites, I came across a nonprofit called *Future Doctors for South Sudan,* founded by Dr. Kenneth Waxman. My heart rate shot up as I read about the program. Dr. Ken had been to South Sudan in 2010 on assignment with *Doctors without Borders* in California. Compelled by the severe lack of access to health care in a largely rural country, he wanted to help. One year before my country gained independence, Dr. Ken established his non-profit to fundraise in support of medical students financially stranded and unable to complete their education. There was one non-negotiable condition—students receiving scholarship funds must plan on practicing in South Sudan.

That was me. I opened the PDF application.

14

PRESENT DAY

Nyal, South Sudan

It was five o'clock in the evening. My staff and I prepared to leave the clinic and return to our residences. It had been a long day. I had just finished progress notes on the last of my patients when a commotion distracted me. Selina, my assistant, was leading a pregnant woman clearly in labour into one of the treatment rooms. I followed them. Martina's history revealed that she had had thirteen live births. Now forty-five years old, she was in labour on her fourteenth. At first all seemed well until she told us that seven of those thirteen children had died before the age of five. "Unknown disease" was what Martina understood as the cause of death. Seven times. She did mention that each child had suffered a high fever before death. Sadly, that was not uncommon. Martina's children, like many in South Sudan, died either at home, be that a village or in the bushes surviving war. In none of the seven deaths were any health services available.

Martina was optimistic about her current pregnancy, having regularly attended antenatal clinic at our facility beginning in the second trimester. Our midwife, Selina, who oversaw the antenatal care, was much loved by the community for her dedication to each patient. Pregnant moms had no difficulty trusting her. Martina was no exception. Like many expectant mothers in Nyal, this would be the first time she would deliver her baby in a health care facility. Selina had explained the protocol to her—come to the clinic as soon as labour starts.

After taking Martina's history, I instructed Selina to do a physical assessment. A few minutes later she reported back to me—Martina's cervix was dilated to about two centimeters, the fetal heart rate strong at 124 beats/minute, all maternal vital signs within the normal range.

It would be an easy night with no signs of complications, and no guilt in my handing responsibilities over to my staff so I could get some sleep. As Selina finished plotting Martina's numbers on the pantograph so we could track changes, the night midwife arrived to begin her shift. Selina gave her a brief report, and off we both went, leaving Martina in good hands.

In my dream someone was pounding a drum in the distance. Then it stopped. But it started again. This time I opened my eyes. It was not a drum, nor was it a dream. Someone was definitely pounding my door. I squinted at the clock. Any clinician will tell you that being awakened at four in the morning is never a good sign.

"Doctor Onyango!" It sounded like our gate keeper, Zacharia. I opened the door a crack.

"Come, Doctor...come to the clinic!"

I pulled on jeans and a tee shirt. In a half-run behind Zacharia, my mind raced through the possibilities. Complications—a mom in labour must be experiencing complications. In the one minute it took us to reach the clinic, a memory flashed through my mind, one that still haunted me, popping into my head in quick flashes that pulled me in.

Her name was Elizabeth, a twenty-three-year old mother of two. Those children had been delivered at home without incident. It had been late afternoon when we caught sight of them—about twenty men slogging their way up the muddy road toward the clinic. Four men carried a stretcher made of wooden poles and cloth. Locals bringing a patient by stretcher meant only one thing—the patient was severely ill. In the rainy season women had to walk many hours to reach the clinic, and they did. This woman could not. Even had a car been available, the rainy season turned the road into a sea of mud, impassable. By the time she reached our clinic, the men had been carrying Elizabeth for ten hours.

Selina and I had rushed out to meet them. The men helped us get her into an exam room. From her history, Elizabeth had been in labor at home for five days. She was extremely dehydrated, and her urinary bladder was full, distended. The labia were seriously inflamed. On exam her cervix was fully dilated. But the baby had not descended. That could only mean one thing—obstructed labour. Elizabeth needed a Cesarean Section. Without one she would die. Our clinic was not set up for surgical procedures, and the hospital was miles away, too far to walk in an emergency. We knew it. The men knew it.

I had started an IV and given normal saline and dextrose to hydrate her and bring her blood sugar up to boost her energy for what lay ahead. We emptied her bladder. Other than trying to stabilize this mother, there was little we could do without surgical intervention. We had one long shot.

I was scheduled to go by car to Torit that day. A vehicle would be waiting for me at the first area accessible by road—a five-hour walk through mud and water. There was no other option. If we had any chance of saving Elizabeth, that car was it. The men had just ended a grueling ten-hour ordeal to reach the clinic. But they were as determined as I was to do everything in my power to save this young mother.

In shifts of four carrying the stretcher, we started out. It was slow going. Heavy mud pulled us down like quicksand, making every step an exhaustive effort. I had instructed the men to set Elizabeth down every thirty minutes so I could assess her condition. For the first two hours—almost halfway to the car—she held her own.

Then our luck ran out. A pool of bloody urine soaked through the cloth stretcher. I told the men to put her down.

On exam, her abdomen was so tender I could easily feel the fetus. The uterus had ruptured with massive internal bleeding. We still had at least three hours to get to the car. There was nothing I could do.

I administered saline to keep her hydrated. It was no use. Her face turned pale as the life drained out of her. I went numb. I was watching Likali die all over again. The defeat I felt was the same as it had been with my sister. I was a child back then. But as a doctor, I knew what my patient needed. It didn't matter. She would not get her emergency C-section.

Had it been the dry season we might have saved her life. This was the cruel reality of rural South Sudan. I was helpless to save this young mother. Time ran out. We gathered around her in silence. All I could do was watch. Thirty minutes later Elizabeth was dead. This terrible memory lasted only a few seconds as I trotted alongside Zacharia. But the flashback always brought up the same questions. Could I have done more? Done something different? In my head I knew our effort had been hopeless—the woman had already been carried by litter for ten hours to get to me. Another five just to get to the car that would transport her to the hospital had been a losing proposition before we started.

I had not failed Elizabeth. South Sudan had failed her, and every other mother whose life or that of her child had been lost due to lack of access to care. Yes, that was what my brain repeated. But my heart would not let go.

Zacharia held the clinic door for me. As we rushed inside, I shoved the traumatic memory of Elizabeth out of my mind. I needed every bit of focus for whatever waited for me in the exam room. *Please God, don't let it happen again.* I went in. The midwife on duty explained that she could not pick up a fetal heart tone.

I turned to Zacharia. "Call Selina." With twenty years of experience, Selina was the first one the nurses would call if there was extreme trouble. Martina lay watching our faces as we bustled about. She rattled off a series of questions, none of which I could answer until we figured out what was happening. Commanding my heart to stop pounding in my ears, I listened for fetal heart tones. Nothing. I looked at Selina. With her stethoscope tight on Martina's belly, she listened as well. No heart tones. Selina and I exchanged glances. Silence filled the room. I listened again. One midwife managed to calm Martina so the other could do an exam. Martina was dilated to eight centimeters, her vital signs normal. But contractions had stopped.

The baby was dead. It still had to be delivered. I ordered Oxytocin to stimulate contractions. Then I was prepared to answer the questions my patient had been asking, though she already knew the answer to the one she did not want to hear. Martina was stoic. Like all of us, she had seen so much death—babies, our elders, men in their prime cut down in war. I gave her what comfort I could, suppressing frustration that we had no access to emergency care.

By seven in the morning there was no sign of the baby coming. I told Selina to remain and monitor Martina while I went home to freshen up before returning to do rounds. When I came back at eight-thirty, Martina had delivered a fresh stillborn baby. Selina assured me that everything was okay. I told her to go freshen up while the night shift midwife was still on site to monitor Martina, as she would after a live birth. Delivery is really a two-part process, the baby, and the placenta. Both are delivered, though no one cares about the afterbirth except labor and delivery staff. Martina's placenta still had to come out, all of it. That would happen shortly with the stillborn now delivered. I left my patient in good hands, then returned to the ward to finish rounds.

It was noon when I heard someone shout my name from down the hall. Selina. It was an urgent scream. Rushing to the maternity ward, I went straight to Martina's room. She lay soaked in a pool of blood, gasping for breath. Selina inserted an intravenous cannula—bigger than a regular IV, which was not sufficient to rapidly administer fluids to compensate for the blood she had lost. I told Selina to get as much normal saline in as fast as she could.

With a dangerously low blood pressure of 60/40, Martina was deathly pale, her pulse weak. She was sweating profusely, her extremities cold—all signs she was going into shock. Her entire circulatory system was shutting down, blood loss of such a volume that her heart might no longer pump enough oxygen to vital organs, including her brain.

As Selina and I worked in unison, Martina lost consciousness. The IV fluids were not keeping up with the blood loss. It was Elizabeth all over again.

Then it came to me. I turned to Selina. "Part of the placenta must still be in her uterus." I began inspecting Martina's cervix. "You saw it all come out...right?"

For a moment Selina did not answer. Then with a sidelong glance, her voice taut, she did. "Not...I mean...not all of it."

I squinted at her, pressing for more information.

"I removed a lot of pieces manually...but...not all of it, I guess."

Copious amounts of bright fresh blood oozed out of Martina's cervix along with dark lumps—the clots. I had to get the remaining tissue out. Inserting my fingers further into the uterus, displacing more clots, I manually evacuated as best I could. But the bleeding continued. With my whole right hand in her uterus, I tried to evacuate the rest. But Martina's cervix was closing fast. I could not reach the uterine wall with my hand. It was hopeless. Panic stirred in my chest.

Wait! The vacuum! Of course! A manual aspiration kit would suction the clots out of her womb. And we had one! It took me less than sixty seconds to insert a speculum into her cervix, passing the thin vacuum tube into the uterus. Satisfied that it was in place, I grabbed the handheld syringe and began to suction. Bits of tissue and clots came out, but the bleeding continued. Martina, still unconscious, was spared the cramping that would have accompanied this process.

Selina and I glanced at each other with the same thought. Never had I been aware of how time gets distorted during a crisis, everything happening in slow motion. It felt like an eternity, but at last the bleeding stopped. Martina opened her eyes. I glanced at the clock to make note of how long she had been unconscious. It had been ten minutes since I walked in the room. Ten of the longest minutes of my life. I smiled at Martina, her face pale as death. But she was very much alive.

Our moment of relief was fleeting. Martina needed a blood transfusion. Our facility was not set up for that. A clinic run by an international rescue group did have blood transfusion services. It was a three-hour drive, but after stabilizing her, Martina would be strong enough for transport. I made the referral.

Watching the transport vehicle drive away, a mix of emotions came over me—relief that Martina had not died; satisfaction in how I handled the crisis; gratitude that our rural clinic was equipped with a vacuum kit. By a slender thread, we had saved our patient. Relief was followed by an overwhelming sense of dismay.

Martina had been fortunate to have health services nearby where she could be under the care of a midwife during her pregnancy, a midwife who had instructed her to come to the clinic when she went into labour. Fortunate that she had survived a life-threatening complication because the clinic had a basic piece of equipment. Fortunate that as a new doctor I had been fast on my feet and pulled every-thing together for a positive outcome.

Five days later we got word that Martina had recovered. Had Martina been at home, she would have died along with her baby. A live mother with a dead baby. In South Sudan, that is our bitter half-measure of success. Is it any wonder that this is one of the deadliest places in the world to give birth with little access to a facility? Home births often include the use of a sharp instrument to cut the umbilical cord. That instrument is usually contaminated. UNICEF had introduced a toxoid vaccine campaign for women of child-bearing age to prevent neonatal tetanus.

Yes, tetanus. Our needs are that basic.

The final case I will tell you about perfectly illustrates this urgent need for services. It happened in Lafon, at the health center where I was doing family planning training. A girl named Josephine would become another extraordinary patient memory, both in her delivery and the unimaginable difficulty of saving her life.

Fourteen years old, Josephine had come into the clin-ic complaining of urinary burning and pain, a telltale sign of infection. Indeed, her labs confirmed it. She was also 36 weeks pregnant. The fetal heart tone was good. I treated her infection and off she went. Three days later she was back. This time in labour. I admitted her. Later that afternoon Josephine said she had felt a funny pop. I assumed that was the natural progression of labour into Stage Two, the rupture of her amniotic membrane. But when I examined her, the baby was presenting—hand-first—in medical terms, hand prolapse. The baby's hand was literally pushing against the vagina. This is a rare occurrence, a very dangerous complication for delivery.

One thing was clear. The baby could not be delivered at the clinic. Josephine needed a Cesarian Section, which meant she had to get to a hospital.

Of course it was during the rainy season, between May and November. Two lives were on the line with the road inaccessible. I put in a call to the Torit office requesting a vehicle be sent to the first accessible place near the clinic, about 8 kms/ 5 miles away. Josephine would have to be carried by litter. Three days after I put in the request, I got a call. The car had been dispatched—but it was stuck in the mud 30 km/18 miles from the clinic. I had seen many cars pulled out of mud. But now, instead of the shorter distance we had planned to carry Josephine, the locals we hired would have to carry her 30 km/18 miles. By then the car would be ready.

Below left: me in the center.

The IV was carried on a pole along side Josephine.

Me checking the IV fluid level.

I listened for heart tones every 30 minutes

Our team started out at eight in the morning for the long walk. Joska, one of our midwives came along as well. Josephine handled the distance as well as could be expected. On arrival at the vehicle, we all stopped in unison. It was sunk deep in mud. The men had not been able to dislodge it. A tractor had arrived. But for the moment, no one was going anywhere.

Four hours later we were still waiting. It was becoming clear that no way was that car coming out of the mud anytime soon. Still, I wasn't ready to give up on the tractor. There was just no way we could walk all the way to the hospital. Two hours later, I got word that *Save the Children,* an NGO active in the area, had ordered a car to a place called Imehejek, a three-hour walk from where we were. I called the clinic to track down the driver's number. When I reached him, he called his boss, who approved our emergency rescue.

By this time it was already night, our 30 km/18 mile trek eating up most of the day, followed by the three hours we spent waiting for the car to be pulled from the mud, then another two arranging transport with *Save the Children's* car. Now we would be walking an additional three hours. But at least we would have a vehicle. We started walking. It was midnight when we arrived in imehejek, sixteen hours after leaving the clinic that morning.

You can imagine my relief at having gotten Josephine safely to the hospital. On arrival, the medical officers on duty examined her. But the doctor detected no fetal heart tone. That was impossible! I had just examined her before we arrived and there had indeed been a fetal heart tone. The doctor responded with a blank stare. I bent over Josephine with my stethoscope. The fetal heart tone was weak, but no question, it was there. They could go ahead with the C-section.

But no. They would not budge. My findings must be a mistake, wishful thinking, they said. I begged the doctor to do an emergency C-section to save the mother's life. He responded that it was not an emergency and could wait until the next day. There was another reason he wanted to defer the surgical delivery—there were no lights in their operating theater.

I was devastated. After all our effort, Josephine's baby would die. I had no choice but to wait it out. This was health-care in rural South Sudan. Something as straightforward as a Cesarian Section could not be performed because the hospital lacks basic infrastructure—lights in the OR.

Early in the morning, they did do the C-section. To their great shock, the baby's heart was beating! I let out a cry of joy, unable to hide relief that both Josephine and her baby made it. My midwife Joska and I named the boy Emmanuel, which means "God is with us."

There is no doubt that God had been with us that day with Josephine in distress during our sixteen-hour journey getting to the hospital and waiting through the night.

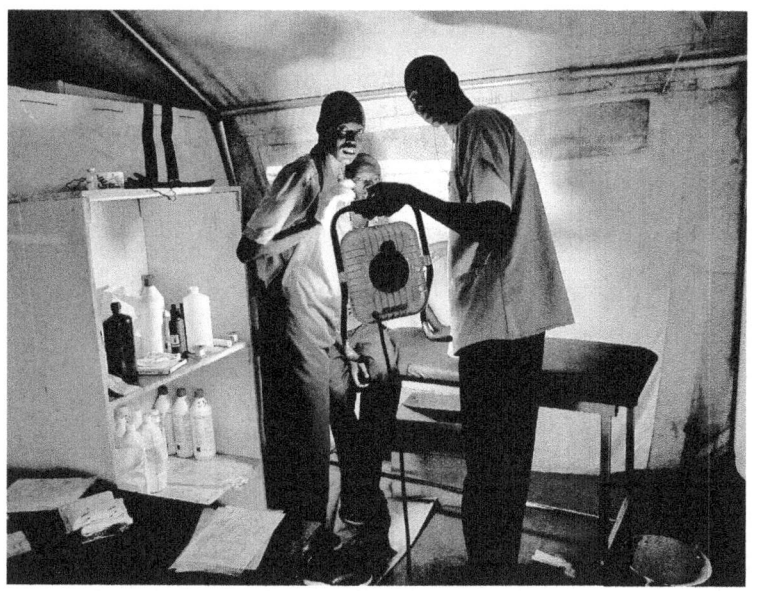

Dinka men holding OR lights.
Courtesy of Kenneth Waxman, M.D. Gogrial, 2010.

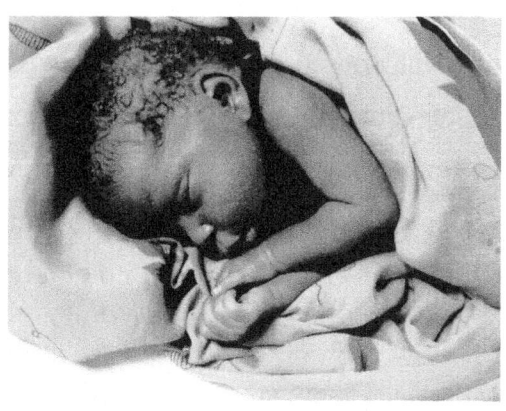

Photo courtesy of Kenneth Waxman, M.D., Gogrial, 2010.

Josephine's delivery had been the most dramatic experience I had faced in my short career, the unimaginable difficulty of saving her life with a dangerous complication in the remote village of Lafon during the rainy season. This is the situation I live with every day, the reality I struggle to accept as a physician in our mostly rural country. I know what the patient needs, I know how to accomplish it. The roadblocks to better outcomes are extremely frustrating. How long will South Sudan depend on organizations like UNICEF because we lack basic infrastructure—trained doctors and nurses, clinics, technicians and equipment, to say nothing of adequate transport for emergencies in a country with no paved roads outside the capital city of Juba, no access at all during the rainy season in places like my clinic in Nyal, or in Lafon.

How long will women travel hundreds of miles, days, even weeks on foot to reach a clinic? Or be carried by family? How many will continue to die on the way? How many Martinas will lose their babies? How many Elizabeths will we lose in childbirth when no emergency care is available?

My goal of saving South Sudan's next generation to build a better country had never been in reach. I knew that. What

I had not known was the challenge of saving one mother, one child, some days a Herculean task. I think about my generation, how many have been lost to the ravages of war and the poverty left in its wake. How long will it take to recover from that?

Will we have a functional health care system by the time my young siblings are having families? What about our educational system that has been left in tatters with a floundering government? How long until jobs are available for refugees still living in camps—like my family—so they can rebuild their lives and live independently?

When colleagues learn that I grew up in a refugee camp, they often respond with shock. I have lived through and witnessed decades of war and its effect on ordinary villagers. The fighting continues to this day as we struggle to survive tribal warfare for control of our government. Food scarcity is a fact of life. At least in Kakuma we had enough to survive, basic healthcare, education. Today in South Sudan many still do not.

As a young country there are huge obstacles to overcome for all of us, but especially for the generation coming of age right now. The ongoing conflict will end. Then it will be up to the next generation to build a better country where we can find our way to peace and a national identity that retains our tribal heritage while moving forward as part of the global community in the twenty first century. There are monumental obstacles ahead for South Sudan.

But obstacles can be overcome. I should know.

EPILOGUE

Last January, twenty-five years after first arriving in Kakuma, I was able to move my mom, Udong, Achii, Akoo, and Anur from the refugee camp in Kenya to a rented house in a town called Eldoret. Udong finished high school in 2013. University was financially impossible. He got a job teaching at the school in Kakuma, and that experience made it clear to him that teaching was his path forward. Today with my financial support he is at university pursuing a bachelor's degree.

Achii is ready for university as well. Like Udong, my sister graduated high school in Kakuma and became a teacher. Also like our brother, Achii dreams of pursuing a degree in the field of education. This fall, in 2020, with my savings I will be able to finance her degree at university.

Akoo is still in high school, Form 2, doing well. Anur is in Form 1. That gives me time to save for their future.

THE END

ACKNOWLEDGMENTS

There is no way I can adequately express my heartfelt gratitude to all those who have helped me throughout my education from the time I was twelve years old. I wonder how many people would bet on any child of twelve in a refugee camp who dreamed of becoming a doctor, much less a girl in a country where education for girls was not valued. Father Elia was the first to put his belief in me. I am also grateful to Father Matthew for supporting my education at St. Bakhita's after Father Elia's death, a huge gesture of confidence in my ability to succeed. Their belief in me was the strength I drew on facing obstacles large and small on my long journey.

At St. Bakhita's I will also forever be grateful to one very special maths teacher who made it his business to reach out and offer his counsel at a crucial moment when I most needed help. At Stonebic High School, I am grateful to Mariel, one of the Lost Boys of South Sudan, whose incredible story of survival inspired me to keep putting one foot in front of the other. I also thank Mariel for connecting me to the generous man I knew only as 'Mr. Ken' whose foundation provided financial support for me to complete high school.

I owe a debt of gratitude to Dr. Hilary with the Norwegian Church humanitarian program in Lafon. His generous support in "paying it forward" gave me the break I needed to fund most of my years at university and medical school at Mount Kenya in Nairobi. That might have been the end of my dream with no funding for my final year of school had it not been for Dr. Ken Waxman with his nonprofit, *Future Doctors for South Sudan* whose support helped me clear the last major obstacle to completing my medical training. When I filled out the online application, there was never any question of my commitment to serve the people of South Sudan. This is and always will be my home. It was help from *Future Doctors* that not only got me to the finish line but through the gap between school and securing my first post as a physician in Nyal. Dr. Ken and the nonprofit remain a source of encouragement.

The heartbreak of my sister's death, of Father Elia's death, of living in loneliness as a girl away from her family might have crushed my dream at any point during this exhausting journey had it not been for this handful of people. Their involvement went far beyond the financial. Each of them showed unwavering belief in my future, always encouraging me along the way.

I also thank Dr. Ken for connecting me with Lori Windsor Mohr. Lori's willingness to collaborate with me for over two years on this project, writing about a world completely foreign to her, has been a gift—one given for no reason other than belief mine was a story worth telling.

Agwak, education is the path to a better life. My mother's words have never stopped running through my head. I owe everything to her. She gave me stories of a life beyond the confines of our refugee camp, the one she shared with my father before we were driven from our village in Lafon—a world where people lived in peace and health and flourished in their communities. For all the years we wandered South Sudan displaced by war—living in poverty and near starvation—only through her stories did I know of this other world.

Thank you, Mom, for saying 'yes' to Father Elia that Sunday afternoon long ago, for sending me away to St. Bakita's to begin my path to a better future.

ABOUT THE AUTHOR

Dr. Hellen Onyango attended Mount Kenya University, a leading private institution. She graduated in 2017 and completed her internship in general medicine at Thika County Hospital in Kenya, a Level 5 teaching and referral hospital. Currently Hellen is working with Health Link South Sudan as a maternal, neonatal and child health project officer.

And saving to support her younger siblings' dreams.

ABOUT LORI WINDSOR MOHR

Lori Windsor Mohr is an author in Southern California where she lives with her husband and three dogs. Prior to her 23-years of professional writing, Lori taught public health for California State University Dominguez Hills.

Writing with Hellen about her years of struggle has given Lori a deep appreciation for the sheer strength of will Hellen demonstrated in overcoming obstacles beyond Lori's imagination to grasp. Today gender roles continue to be a barrier. According to the United Nations Education Organization, South Sudan still has one of the highest rates of illiteracy in the world with three-quarters of the female population unable to read or write. Hellen's story really is one of extraordinary triumph. Perhaps one day a girl in South Sudan who has a dream that she has been told is impossible will read about a refugee who became a doctor. And perhaps she will be inspired to take the first of countless steps to a better future.

Hellen and South Sudan will always hold a special place in Lori's heart.

SANTA BARBARA LITERARY PRESS

Made in the USA
Coppell, TX
26 November 2020